Now it [?]
one spe [?]

The
Monadnock
Revelations

**A Spiritual
Memoir**

Tom O'Connell

Sanctuary

The Monadnock Revelations:
A Spiritual Memoir

Published in the United States by
Sanctuary Unlimited
P.O. Box 25, Dennisport, MA 02639

For information, address: Sanctuary Unlimited,
Post Office Box 25, Dennisport, MA 02639.

Library of Congress Cataloging in Publication Data
O'Connell, Tom.
The Monadnock Revelations:
A Spiritual Memoir

1. O'Connell, Tom 1932--. 2. Journalists--United
States--Biography. 3. Inspiration. 4. Spiritual life.
5. Mysticism 6. Religious experience.
7. Conduct of life. I. Title.
ISBN 0-9620318-5-2

Library of Congress Catalog Card Number (CIP):
96-92248

**Dedicated
To the God of Love**

**"I love everything.
I love everyone.
I love all,
even those who do not believe."**

--Sept. 5, 1985
Monadnock Mountains

The Monadnock Revelations

Contents...

The Monadnock Revelations:
A Spiritual Memoir
by Tom O'Connell

1
The Quest

This is my story, my truth, and I offer it to you for your consideration. My life has involved a lengthy quest for closer contact with God. And on September 5, 1985, that quest brought me to New Hampshire's Monadnock Mountains where I was guided into a high level of consciousness I had not expected to achieve. I experienced God on that day.

Not only did I have a direct experience of God, I was also given a series of messages by the God of Love to pass on to others who are seeking the divine. I have passed on some of the messages orally, and in my writing, but I now feel motivated to provide this book to communicate more effectively what I learned during the most important hour of my life.

The key message I pass on to you is that God loves us all. Me. You. Everyone. God loves every particle of Creation, and made it clear to me that his love includes those who do not believe. The love of God is inclusive, not exclusive. It belongs to all.

As I tell you the story of my quest, and its results, I hope to get across to you the reality of God's love, as it was expressed during my hour of direct contact.

The Revelations I received in the mountains that day included messages about that love.

Before I outline the Revelations, I will tell you some of my own story. Since my life has been very complicated, I will just give highlights in this book. Obviously, the message is more important than the messenger, but I believe it will help you to know what my life was like before September 5, 1985, and what has been going on with me since that time.

My life, which I think of as a spiritual adventure or journey, has been influenced by many people, and I thank them all for their kindness, understanding, patience, and unconditional love. I am also grateful to other children of God who came before me and took the time to write down their insights so that I could feed my hungry spirit with their words.

As for my direct communication with God in the Monadnock Mountains, I am eternally grateful to two beautiful women who played key roles in the chain of circumstances that led me to Peterborough, New Hampshire, for my time of powerful spiritual awakening. One of these women pointed out the way for me, and I will call her Gloria out of respect for her privacy. The other was Eleanor Moore, the healer and mystic, who gently guided me through the initiation into higher consciousness which is sometimes called the God Experience, and is also described as Christ Consciousness.

Eleanor has gone home to her Creator, the God of Love, but I have a tape of the interview I did with her in January of 1986 when I was seeking to clarify the events of that time of divine communication in her yellow farmhouse in the Monadnock Mountains. She was very helpful to me, her spirit is still with me, and I will quote her tape when I discuss The Monadnock Revelations.

Before I move on with the story, let me say that I believe we are all on the same journey home, yet each of us has a slightly different path to follow. The journey into conscious contact with God is not an easy one, and the quest brings its share of pain, but the joy of spiritual awakening more than offsets any pain felt during the journey to heightened awareness.

Since encounters with adversity have provided important challenges during my journey, the next chapter reviews some of the kinds of adversity that have come my way during this adventure we call life.

2
Familiarity with Adversity

I am very familiar with adversity, and today I see it as a necessary part of my experience. But I've been impatient with adversity, preferring pleasure. I have often resisted the truth that opposing experiences are necessary. I didn't realize then that the adversity in my life was serving a very useful purpose in God's training program for me.

Now I see things differently, and I can relate to the ancient Egyptians who, before initiating a person into highest consciousness, required that the person be able to carry opposing experiences with grace.

The Egyptian initiates were trained to understand the value of silence and talk, caution and courage, humility and self-confidence, detachment and love. They knew of the need to accept the opposing experiences as an integral part of life.

Closer to our time, in 1932, the year I was born, two anonymous women in England got in touch with the spirit world, and their insights were published in *God Calling*. One of their powerful insights, echoing Egyptian thinking, was this phrase: "Appreciation results from contrary experience."

I remind myself of this phrase daily, and as I reflect on my life I try to find something good and useful in each experience. I am grateful not only for pleasant events but also for the times of adversity which have often taught me important lessons.

My first incident of adversity on this planet took place during my birth on February 11, 1932, in a house on Curve Street in Dedham, which is a suburb of Boston. The labor was long and arduous, and affected my mother's mental health.

The postpartum depression Margaret Henderson O'Connell experienced after I was born led to severe psychosis and eventual confinement in a state asylum. Losing her to insanity brought me great grief, but also has given me empathy for all people who have had to face the challenge of having mentally ill parents or other loved ones.

At the age of six months, adversity entered my life again. I suffered a collapsed lung, lost half my body weight, and, according to my father, Thomas Frederick O'Connell, I was brought back from near death to health at Children's Hospital in Boston. It has been obvious to me for a long time that each day since that precarious event has been a gift.

Adversity made its presence felt again when I was two years old. By this time, my mother's mental condition had reached the point where she could not care for me and my younger brother, so we were placed in separate foster homes. On my second birthday, my father learned that my one-year-old brother was gravely ill in the foster home where he had been placed. As it turned out, he had suffered from neglect, and then contracted pneumonia.

Little Jackie died in my father's arms on the way to Children's Hospital, so on the day I became two years old I also became an only child who was treated as an orphan, continued to live in foster care situations, and had no real home. As a result, I have come to deeply appreciate homes of my own, even when I only rent them, and I appreciate whatever health comes to me as a gift from God. I also pray for and appreciate the continuing health of my own four children, their mates, and eight grandchildren.

During those early years of mine, the arrival of adversity had negative effects on my father. To cope with his sadness following the loss of my mother and my brother, he turned to alcohol for solace. And he told me in his later years that his drinking brought him to the point of seriously contemplating suicide.

He told me how he had stood at the end of a pier in Boston Harbor, wondering why he shouldn't end it all. But something stopped him, and I've always been grateful for that. Although he abandoned me to foster care in a group home, I've also been grateful that he retained a connection with me. So I didn't feel completely without family in my early years.

However, the adverse experience of being raised as an orphan in a group foster home left some deep scars on my young psyche. It was not until decades later that I could look back and see that my early training gave me great endurance, resilience, and determination. It also gave me heartfelt empathy for orphans, foster kids, and other displaced people who feel "different." So, on reflection, I can see the divine purpose of the situations that challenged me.

There were other instances of adversity that brought lessons too. The malnutrition I experienced while living with my grandmother during my teens heightened my appreciation for good nutrition. Losing my driver's license during college, because of an incident I did not cause, taught me that even injustice can have a useful result. I certainly learned to appreciate the privilege of driving a car.

Being disabled by infected feet in high school, and having a similar condition resembling trench foot in the army, helped me to appreciate the simple act of walking, and to have empathy for disabled people of all kinds.

Adversity struck again as I was nearing the end of my two years in the U.S. Army. On Christmas Eve 1955, my daughter Peggy became seriously ill due to a viral infection, sank into a coma, and stayed on the brink of death with peritonitis for many days. For a month my wife Mary and I lived with her in a hospital room in Augusta, Georgia, praying for her recovery, and helping out as much as we could with little acts like keeping an eye on her transfusions and intravenous feeding.

At the same time, we were getting a firsthand view of the effects of the polio epidemic that was killing young people in nearby hospital rooms. In a miraculous way, the team of a dedicated pediatrician and skilled surgeons brought our Peggy back to life, even though the odds for doing so were given as one in ten thousand. I will never forget the compassion and generosity we received from those physicians, relatives, friends and strangers who helped us.

As the years passed, I had my share of fun and joy, yet adversity visited repeatedly, always bringing me closer to awareness of God. Today I see adversity as an important piece in the mosaic of my personal history. No painful experience has been useless. All my experiences, pleasurable or painful, have brought lessons. And many of my adverse experiences have nudged me into more suitable directions.

So I believe that the ancient Egyptians had the right idea about carrying the opposite experiences gracefully, and the two anonymous women who connected with the spirit world in 1932 were right on target when they passed on those words to us: "Appreciation results from contrary experience."

I am grateful today for all the experiences that have come my way, whether pleasurable or painful, and I see them as necessary parts of a loving God's plan for my personal development.

Experiencing darkness helps me to appreciate light. Being lonely helps me to appreciate friends and relatives. Living with tension helps me to appreciate peace. Running short of money helps me to appreciate having enough to make ends meet. Experiencing fear helps me to appreciate courage. Being underemployed results in a deep appreciation of satisfactory work. Encountering envy, hate, or indifference helps me to appreciate love. Having had my deep desire to express myself thwarted at various times in my life gives me deep appreciation for this opportunity to share my most personal thoughts and reflections with you. So today I am a very grateful human being, familiar with adversity, and also familiar with joy.

3
Families and Friends

My original family was destined to be fractured, and in my early years I was a transient with no fixed living accommodations. Even before my mother was committed to a state insane asylum, I was living in foster care situations, with relatives or strangers, in the Boston area. According to my father, as his wife's mental condition worsened, his own sense of helplessness grew, and at some point he brought her back to her parents, and left her there. He said her condition continued to deteriorate, and they confined her in their attic. Before reliable psychiatric help was sought, she had retreated into incurable insanity.

The condition and location of my mother were kept secret from me during my childhood, and only in my teens was some information given to me directly. The existence of my mother's family was also a secret. They played no part in my upbringing, and never came to visit me. After my earliest years, I saw neither my mother nor her family until I visited the funeral home after her death when I was nearly forty, and observed my mother's closed casket.

Everything I know about my mother came to me in bits and pieces from my father's stories as the years passed and he recalled earlier times. He said that on our last visit to see her at the state asylum, when I was probably between two and three years old, she took my little body and hurled me across the lobby in an attempt to harm me. My father said that if I had not landed in a potted plant she might have succeeded. That was the last time I saw my mother.

During childhood, my awareness of my mother's condition came to me like pieces in a puzzle, from comments I overheard during my elementary school years. When I finally realized she was in an insane asylum and incurably ill, I felt deep shame. Also, I knew that I couldn't openly discuss this knowledge with anyone, including my closest friends.

As a child I felt abandoned, confused, and very alone even when surrounded by people. Knowing that my mother was insane left me with a fear of insanity, and a question lodged in my own mind about the possibility of going crazy myself. This led to a fear of strong emotions, especially anger, and I became shy and inward as I grew. It took much courage for me to break through my shell of self-protective shyness as an adult.

After living with relatives and strangers up to about age four, I found a more secure place at my grandmother's house in Dedham. Johanna Galvin O'Connell owned a little duplex house next to the East Dedham Railroad Station, in the blighted side of the community, on what used to be called "the other side of the tracks." At 22 Walnut Place, I lived with Granny, my father, and Uncle Joe on one side. Next door lived some of my other relatives. And to round out my sense of belonging to a community, I had friends in the neighborhood. This, I believe, was a time during my childhood when I felt what may be described as a measure of ongoing happiness. Yet deep insecurities remained, and I was subject to awful nightmares throughout my youth.

The time with Granny O'Connell and my father ended when I was five years old. My grandmother was feeling ill and felt she could no longer handle me. Apparently, I gave her a run for her money. An aunt later told me that when I was asked what my name was in those days, I would reply, "Tommy O'Connell, D.P." And when they asked what the D.P. meant, I would say "damn pest."

Although my early years provided a series of traumatic events, I think the lowest point of my emotional life was the day I was driven by my father, in his shiny new black 1937 Plymouth sedan, from Dedham to the nearby town of Norwood. On that day I was being transported to a Catholic Charities group foster home that was run by Margaret White, an Irish immigrant widow who supported herself and her son by taking in boys from broken homes.

I was so furious with my father for abandoning me to 42 Mountain Avenue in Norwood that I vowed at that young age of five never to call him "Dad" again. After all, I thought, a real father would never send me away like that. I kept my promise until I was nearly middle-aged and became able to forgive him for how he had handled my early life. It was difficult not to call him Dad when I lived with him in my teens, but I managed to avoid it.

Also, at age 5, I held back on calling Mrs. White "Mom," which was her chosen name in the house she reigned over like a despotic queen. But after a while I got used to it and accepted her title as a name, if not as reality. Mr. Vincent, a boarder, called her "Margaret," and so did Irish immigrants who stayed at 42 Mountain Avenue for a while on first arriving in the United States. But the boys from Catholic Charities were expected to call her "Mom."

I stayed in Mrs. White's house for nine years, and there were usually half a dozen boys there at any given time. Some stayed for many years; others had shorter stays. All were from broken homes, and most were orphans. As the truth about my mother's condition unfolded, I began to envy the orphans who lived with me. At least their status was clear. I had no mother, and yet she was not dead. And although I had a father alive, he had given me up to foster care. I was an orphan without traditional orphan status, and if this was all part of God's plan for my life, I didn't appreciate the lessons I was learning.

The discipline at Mrs. White's house was often ferocious. I have thought many times that if Hitler had hired her to train his troops, Germany would have won World War II. In fairness though, she was not alone in her physical abuse. In those days severe corporal punishment of children was the accepted practice, and so was mental harassment.

Also, I soon learned that in other foster homes nearby, where young wards of the Commonwealth of Massachusetts lived, living conditions were even more difficult. We Catholic Charities boys were the elite, and we knew that if we got into trouble at Mrs. White's we could end up in far worse circumstances, like the Home of the Angel Guardian in Boston. One of the boys at Mrs. White's had been there, and he had whip scars on his back to show for it. So we tried to live up to her standards.

However, when there was an infringement of her decrees, she would angrily switch us with branches from small trees, shove soap and water solutions down our throats, whap us with wet towels, and knock us across the kitchen with one sweep of her heavy arm. She considered herself a "stout" woman, and she was very strong. When she hit you, you knew it, and her messages had power behind them.

She also put us in dark cellars and dark attics for punishment, and if we broke a major commandment, she would take us by the hair on our heads or pull us by the ears, and march us down cellar to the toilet there, and shove our heads down into the toilet bowl, flush the toilet so that it would irrigate the various openings in our heads, and continue this process until we gagged and became very repentant.

I hated her punishment techniques, especially the humiliating toilet torture, but on the plus side she constantly motivated us to become educated and make the best of ourselves in this life. Even her harsh physical punishment was designed to "put the fear of God" into us, so it wasn't done from evil intentions. I think she was driven by a streak of perfectionism. She was a fanatic about neatness and cleanliness, and she was an excellent cook. Nutrition was exceptional at her house, and she instilled pride into us for being "one of Mrs. White's boys." We were known throughout the community as models of good behavior. And most of the time we were. But we were boys, and far from perfect.

Fortunately, the physical discipline faded when we entered junior high school; then the punishment shifted to losing privileges such as going to the movies or listening to favorite radio programs. It was as if we had survived her rigorous basic training and now could be treated with a modicum of respect.

On reflection, Mrs. White's house was a training ground for industry and productivity. We picked blueberries in the woods and sold them to bakeries, had newspaper routes, and sold raffle tickets for the church. At an early age, all of us earned money caddying at Norfolk Golf Course in Westwood.

Her sense of order was one of her strongest qualities, and each day of her week had its purpose. Wash day. Ironing day. Cleaning day. Marketing day. Yard maintenance day. Baking day. Prayer day.

Another positive aspect of Mrs. White's house was the religious training. She was an Irish Roman Catholic with strong convictions, and we practiced the faith with no shortcuts. She thought about God constantly, respected God, and talked about the presence of God endlessly.

Jesus Christ was real in that house, and so were Jesus's mother Mary and foster father Joseph. We learned that our purpose in life was to know, love, and serve God in this world and to be happy with God in the next, and whenever I have forgotten that in later years I have not been a happy person.

I remember how we lined up our chairs in the kitchen, with the backs toward the table, and how she had us kneel on the chair seats as she led us in reciting the Rosary. She also made sure we went to Holy Communion every Sunday, with confession preceding it on Saturday afternoons in the chapel behind St. Catherine's Church. And during Lent we went to Mass daily. Those of us who went to the public schools, then described as "the Protestant schools," had to go to the parochial school for instruction on Sunday mornings after Mass.

Beyond this, I developed my own relationship with church and God. I prayed to my God constantly, and although most other boys thought of church as a place for enforced prayer, I went on my own to St. Catherine's to perform solitary "holy hours." I loved that place of dark mahogany and colorful stained glass, especially when I was alone in the silence directly communicating my young thoughts to God.

In Sunday school I received all A's, and had perfect attendance for all nine years. Similarly, at Cornelius M. Callahan elementary school I received all A's for six years, and there I was known as the smartest boy. So, although I had deficits in my early life, I also had the pride of achievement.

Anxious to learn to read, I had asked friends in my neighborhood in East Dedham to teach me the alphabet long before I went to school. From the earliest times I had a love affair with books and words. One of my favorite stories was *The Little Engine That Could.* And its message still inspires me. I believe that with determination each human being can tap into amazing capabilities, and the key ingredient in life is willingness to stretch beyond the ordinary. In addition to motivational reading, I also devoured entertaining fiction. It was like therapy for me. I could always escape into a good book.

Even though I was shy, I liked school right from the start, and I believe the teachers appreciated my intelligence and quiet manner. I was the boy they chose to bring important messages to the school principal's office, and I thrived on being responsible.

Mrs. White used to describe me as "refined," and I was one of the boys who was least likely to get into trouble. Yet I inwardly questioned her authority.

Frankly, I resented it deeply, and since those days I've had difficulty with arbitrary authority. But to avoid punishment I conformed. Survival was the name of the game, and being intelligent, I foresaw the consequences of my own behavior and usually avoided self-destructive actions.

So I operated as an inner rebel and an outward conformist while feeling like a prison inmate with an indefinite sentence. Then, after spending six years at Mrs. White's house, I received one of the major disappointments of my life. The two boys who were my best friends at the foster home, Dave and Joe Rothwell, were returning to their home in the Hyde Park section of Boston when they finished the sixth grade. And this motivated me to ask my father if I could go back home to Dedham to live with him and Granny O'Connell. Asking him was very anxiety-provoking, but I prayed about it, requested God's help with it, got up my courage, and asked. The answer was no, and I felt crushed.

My father said I would have to stay with Mrs. White for three more years, until I finished Norwood Junior High. Very unhappy with this turn of events, I faced the loss of my two best friends with deep sadness, and began to feel like a prisoner who had just had three years added to his sentence. I reacted with a blend of frustration, anger, and depression.

Soon I began spending more time across the street with my friend John Flaherty. I studied less, and took up smoking and swearing. I even tried some minor thievery at the local Five and Ten Cent store. But I was a very poor thief, and not adept at smoking. I could swear well though, and learned how to combine vulgarity and sarcasm. My habitual swearing continued until I heard a Jesuit professor at Boston College describe swearing as "the sign of a lazy mind." And I didn't want that label, so I quit.

Looking back at my early teens, it's clear to me that I became less of a perfectionist and less of an idealist. In junior high, I purposely descended from being an A student to the level of B, and told myself I was tired of being "an egghead." Actually, I began taking it easy in all aspects of my life. I even moved so slowly that the gym teacher called me "Old Man O'Connell." And I continued my hobby of reading novels, usually mysteries and adventure stories.

Finally, at age 14, I was permitted to leave Mrs. White's house and return to Granny O'Connell's duplex in East Dedham, where I would stay until my early twenties. However, the first summer of my new freedom was spent caddying at Saranac Inn in the Adirondacks, along with my friends Dave and Joe Rothwell. That was when I experienced various rites of passage including my first alcoholic beverage, gambling at cards, and an attempt at having a girl friend. I was instantly allergic to the alcohol, and so embarrassed by the outcome that I didn't drink again until I was 17 years old. I was not a good gambler. And I was no great shakes as a young lover either.

When I showed up at Granny's duplex in time to begin my sophomore year at Dedham High School, I felt mature, and was happy I no longer had to say, "I live with Mrs. White." But as I settled in at Granny's house, it was obvious that the standard of living in the foster home had been much higher. And I had developed habits of neatness and cleanliness that did not exist in Granny's little duplex in the soot laden neighborhood next to the old railroad station. As a result, my life with Granny was a battle of wits, or maybe I should say a contest of wills.

However, at Granny's I was free to do just about anything I pleased. My father was busy with his own life, working long hours in the U.S. Post Office, and had minimum involvement in my life although we shared living quarters. My uncle Joe spent some time there too, between clerical jobs in Washington, D.C. Granny, who seemed very old to me, spent her time in her rocking chair praying and commenting to herself on the news of the day. An avid radio listener, she debated with news commentators, and I would make wisecracks about her points of view.

Living at Mrs. White's, I had been well fed and clothed. At Granny's I wore obvious patches on my socks and underwear, and my nutrition was at the malnutrition level. But I was free to roam without supervision, hung around the poolroom in East Dedham Square observing tough boys and men at play, studied at the Dedham Public Library, and spent much time with new friends while also having friends in the Walnut Place neighborhood which I had visited over the years on brief vacations.

At Dedham High, the three boys I became very close to were Fran Currie, Mike Eremita, and John Kohut. Fran's heritage was primarily Irish, Mike's parents had emigrated from Italy, and John's family was Polish. Whereas Norwood had been a large Irish ghetto, with one section of town called Dublin and another called Cork City, Dedham had a much more mixed population. At Mrs. White's we were exposed to "There are only two kinds of people, the Irish and those who want to be," and "There's no place like Norwood." In Dedham the viewpoint was broader.

After moving to Dedham, I visited Mrs. White every so often, and we became friends. As time passed, her good qualities were more apparent since I could see her realistically after leaving her domain. She was an exceptional woman, and her positive attitude about higher education helped motivate me to aim for entrance to Boston College. But even though I respected her, and had higher living standards at her house, I preferred being with my own family where I had a degree of freedom not available to most 14-year-old boys. I treasured that freedom. It was my most important possession.

At 22 Walnut Place, in Granny's house, life was uncomfortable. There was no central heating, as at Mrs. White's. Instead, the only heat came from an oil stove in the kitchen and a kerosene space heater in the living room that would leak its flaming fluid onto the rug periodically. The bedrooms upstairs were unheated, and ice cold in the winter. The single bathroom shared by occupants of both sides of the house was like a refrigerator. However, there was hot water for the tub in the winter, whereas only cold water ran from spring through fall unless we heated some on the hotplate on top of the kitchen stove, which didn't operate during temperate weather.

Next door, on the other side of Granny's duplex, my Uncle Bill and Aunt Rita were developing a rapidly expanding young family. It was fun living in the same house with my cousins and watching them grow. They provided an energy next door that could be easily heard through the walls of the old house.

A short distance down the street from Walnut Place was East Dedham Square, which had more taverns in a smaller area than most locations around

Boston. In that square I learned about the depressed side of human existence, and also learned that in the middle of what seems like the worst situation there are glimmers of the best. At an early age I learned about the contrast between light and darkness, and how one needs the other. I also learned to reserve judgment on my fellow human beings while trying to discern their character traits as objectively as I could.

At Granny's, without Mrs. White's discipline, I was less rigid in my religious practice, and never let St. Mary's Parish know I was at 22 Walnut Place in Dedham and eligible for religious instruction classes. I had received the sacrament of Confirmation at St. Catherine's in Norwood, and saw no need for similar instruction in Dedham. Also, I stopped attending Mass every day during Lent, and went to confession less often. But I rarely missed Mass on Sundays and Holy Days, loved the mystical sounds and feelings of the Latin rite, and I said my own daily prayers.

In high school, I used the sophomore year as a vacation from serious studying, and the next year I buckled down, went onto the Honor Roll, and began earning the grade averages necessary to be accepted at Boston College, the only institution of higher education that interested me. Becoming active in school activities, I played on the Golf Team, wrote for the Yearbook, took a small part in the Senior Play, and became School Champion in the Spelling contest sponsored by the Boston Herald.

During my senior year of Dedham High, my father left his job in the Post Office and went with a colleague, Hazel Berg, to Wells, Maine, to develop a motor court for tourists. Again he was separating himself from me, but although I missed him some, I didn't miss him much. There was a part of me that felt very unwelcome in his life. Even while living with me, he had spent most of his hours at work, at race tracks, or with friends.

Anyhow, I enjoyed being independent. But when my father was not around, the diet always got worse. Granny survived on tea and toast. And rarely was my hunger satisfied during the years I lived with her. On the other side of the coin though, when my father was gone I had my own private bedroom. Granny always slept downstairs on a cot in the dining room.

Eventually, my father and Hazel were married, after he had obtained a Las Vegas divorce from my institutionalized mother. Starting a second family in Maine, he fathered five girls and a boy after the age of 45, and because of the distance between us I described the new group as "my father's kids."

As it turned out, his motor court venture in Maine spawned financial pressure that curbed my plans to go to college. In the spring of 1949, when I told him I had been accepted at Boston College, I was saddened when he said he had taken the money Granny had saved to help me start college and used it for the new business. He said he would help me when he was able to, indicated that someday I would benefit from his enterprise, and said I'd have to find myself a job in the fall instead of going to college.

Then he invited me to spend the summer of 1949 in Maine, to help out during the first season of the motel business. I agreed, and after I graduated from Dedham High School, I went to Wells, Maine, and helped a bit. I say "a bit" because I readily admit that I was not a rugged type who loved manual labor. I was about six feet tall, extremely thin, and fatigued easily, so my energy expenditure was not high. The junior high gym teacher had not been exaggerating when he had called me "Old Man O'Connell."

While in Maine I studied for my driver's license exam, and was trained by my father's brother-in-law Russell Berg who, at that time, was operating on a license suspension. That didn't keep him from taking me out on the highways of Maine and teaching me to drive even though he was risking severe punishment if we were stopped by the State Police.

Later in the summer I took the exam in Norwood, Massachusetts, managing to get my license even though I ran a red light during the test when the sun's glare distorted my vision. Shortly after that, my father talked Russell into letting me have the 1934 Plymouth he was no longer using. This was my transportation from then on. So there I was, finished with high school, in possession of my license to drive, and the owner of my own car at the age of 17.

At the same time I was feeling the glow of young manhood, I was also feeling very lonely that summer in Maine. As I reflect, it's apparent to me that during my early years I lived a lone wolf existence much of the time. And I never shared the truth about my loneliness with anyone. Admitting loneliness, or any other weakness one had, just wasn't done. Strength and courage were the standard values in those days, and young men even avoided sharing their fears and concerns with close friends.

Because I had no friends my own age in Maine, I was eager to get back home with my pals. We had become very close during our high school years together, had a shared sense of humor, and enjoyed each other's company. So, after Labor Day, it was back to Dedham where it felt good to be with my pals again. But it didn't feel so wonderful to look ahead to a year of manual labor instead of continuing on with my higher education. And I was concerned about the gap between high school and Boston College. But I was determined not to let anything or anybody get in the way of my pursuit of a liberal arts education. I was fixed on that goal.

Frustrated by my father's negative impact on my timetable, I went to work at the Boston Envelope Company at the lowest level, earning 90 cents an hour. Fortunately, Granny really came through for me, allowing me to live at her place without paying board. So I was able to save most of my pay, other than what I needed to keep the 15-year-old car functioning. During that year of hard work at the factory, I used hydraulic jacks to bring heavy pallets of paper to machines, and later filled the role of shipping clerk. In this venture into the world of factory production, I punched a time clock, learned about a slice of life that was shared by many ordinary people, saved money, spent time with my friends, and read the books that attracted my attention at the Dedham Public Library.

Then in the spring of 1950 my father asked me for a loan from the tuition money I had been saving. His request truly gave me the horrors, because I had minimal trust in his ability to honor agreements with me. But because he was my father I loaned him most of what he wanted, holding back enough to get me started at Boston College in the fall. His slowness in repaying me increased my level of financial as well as emotional stress during the early years of college, but eventually he made up for the deficiency.

4
Opening the Mind

As my freshman year at Boston College opened in the fall of 1950, I was a young man whose dream had come true. This had truly been the college of my choice, and from my earliest years I had aspired to attend B.C. I was so determined to go there I had not applied for admission anywhere else.

So there I was, in this Jesuit institution of higher learning, surrounded by gothic buildings reminiscent of medieval times, beginning my classical education in the College of Arts and Sciences.

There was a lump in my throat on that first day, and mist in my eyes. It was a bit unreal to think that I had been raised in a Catholic Charities group foster home, and then had spent years in Granny's old duplex next to the East Dedham railroad station, and had been working in a factory for a year, and was now a peer of boys who had gone to Boston College High and various prep schools so they could qualify for B.C., primarily a men's college then.

My emotional reaction included gratitude and awe. And there was no question in my mind about the correctness of my choice. Boston College and I had a mystical connection, right from the start. The motto at B.C., "Ad Majorem Dei Gloriam," meant "For the Greater Glory of God." I felt that message deeply, and on the campus I found a beautiful chapel where I could go to pray frequently.

At Boston College in those days there was little choice of electives. Pursuing the bachelor of arts curriculum, we had as many courses in philosophy and theology as we had in our majors, and I thrived on the diet. I chose History and Government as my major, and also studied higher mathematics, physics, French, Latin, economics, and courses such as poetry and rhetoric. I was most fascinated by philosophy and theology because they reached parts of my spirit that other subjects could not touch.

As my freshman year opened I was confident in my ability to do well at B.C. Although I had been out of high school for nearly a year and a half, I had not been on a vacation from books. My hobby of reading novels had continued unabated, and authors I was following in those days were Dostoyevsky, F. Scott Fitzgerald, and Hemingway. For nonfiction I enjoyed humorist Rube Goldberg. And Robert Benchley, who wrote *My Ten Years in a Quandary and How They Grew*, was one of my favorite writers.

I enjoyed the mental regimen at the Heights and became a consistent Dean's List student. Feeling at home on the beautiful Chestnut Hill campus, I did a large amount of my studying in the Bapst Library. In those days B.C. was primarily a commuter college, and I was one of many students who came to the college each day, studied in the library between classes, and returned home in the evening. Only a small group of boys lived in dormitories on campus.

When I started at Boston College a new building was being developed, to complete a quadrangle. It was called the Philosophy Building. When the work was done, there above its center arch were these words: "You will come to know the truth and the truth will set you free." Those words became a vital part of my conscious life.

Other words inspired me too. There was the poem "Invictus" by William Ernest Henley: "I am

the master of my fate: I am the captain of my soul."
And the voice of conscience expressed in Francis
Thompson's "The Hound of Heaven" also stayed with
me: "I fled Him, down the nights and down the days;
I fled Him, down the arches of the years; I fled Him,
down the labyrinthine ways of my own mind...." I
tried to flee from God's will many times, but no
matter where I tried to run, God was always there to
remind me of his presence.

Although I loved Boston College, and was among
the top group of students scholastically, my years of
studying there were stressful. The diet at Granny's
house remained at the malnutrition level, and I also
had to work constantly at low paying part-time jobs.
I worked in grocery stores and soda fountains, and
sold magazines. Another place where I worked was
Massachusetts Osteopathic Hospital, buffing floors
and incinerating the surgical leftovers on weekends
and holidays. Not a pleasant task.

During summers I worked with a contractor as a
carpenter, along with my high school pals, and we
built houses west of Boston. I tried to save as much
money as I could during the vacation period, but also
did my share of drinking alcohol and "burning the
candle at both ends," as Granny used to say, which
surely had an adverse effect on my health.

To help myself financially, I attracted a small
scholarship from the Father Fleming Scholarship
Fund at St. Mary's parish in Dedham, and Granny
O'Connell helped from time to time, as did my
father. But, for the most part, I worked my own way
through college. And at one point I considered
joining the U.S. Marine Reserve Officers Training
Corps to get my tuition paid, pending agreement to

serve in the Marines after graduation. However, I failed the physical because of high blood pressure and an anxiety state. My pulse was racing.

As I approached junior year, my health was in jeopardy. I had functioned as long as I could with no energy stores in reserve, and I began to experience a cluster of frightening symptoms. Heart palpitations. Racing heart. Muscular twitches. Dizzy spells. And general weakness. Doctor Moran, the family doctor, suggested rest but I couldn't conceive of dropping out of college to restore my health. So I continued to maintain high grades and exhaust myself because I did not understand my own limits. Also, I treasured the moments at Boston College, and couldn't imagine changing my plans.

During that third year of college I fell in love with Mary Killoren, who had also been raised in Norwood, and I began to see the possibility of taking some time away from college after my junior year. I devised a plan to leave college, notify the Draft Board in Dedham that I was no longer a student, volunteer to be drafted into the U.S. Army, marry Mary, serve the two years of military service, and complete Boston College later with the aid of the G.I. Bill of Rights. We both agreed on the plan.

5
Marriage and the Military

I left college after the junior year, worked as a timekeeper on a construction project near Columbia Point in Boston, and in November 1953 Mary and I were married. This began a partnership that brought happiness and challenges for many years to come.

Within a month after our marriage we conceived our first child, Peggy, and the following March I was inducted into the Army during the Korean Conflict, which proved to be more of an endurance test than I had anticipated. I had patriotic inclinations but the dehumanizing treatment tortured my independent psyche. Starting out in the Army as a patriot, I soon became a combination of realist and pacifist.

After all, I had been pretty much my own boss since age 14. And I respected education, but not brainwashing. I was fortunate not be invited to a court-martial, since my attitude led me into verbal conflicts with people who ranked higher than I did. As an enlisted man, I began as a buck private, then moved to private first class, and finally became a specialist third class. These were low ranks.

During basic training at Fort Dix, I came down with a case of dermatititis resembling trench foot, and it disabled me for a while, but I managed to finish the Infantry training program and was then assigned to Camp Gordon, Georgia, for Military Police Training. The heat and the humidity in Georgia felt intolerable to me, and so did the new assignment. I was definitely not the police officer type. And my tender feet, still sore from the abuse they had received in basic training, became infected again. But the problem with my feet turned out to be a great blessing.

After hospitalization, I was assigned to a Military Government unit as a clerk-typist, even though I didn't know how to type. Then I began teaching myself to type with a self-teaching manual. Next I asked to attend a special class, and soon could type well. This led to an assignment as feature editor of a small newspaper, *Behind the Eight Ball,* which we developed. I wrote a column, "Ours is Not to Reason Why," which was an outlet for my deep frustration. Later, the Pentagon demanded a less derogatory title and a less cynical masthead. So we became *The MG Gazette,* and my column was titled "Da Men Vich Iss..." This was the way one of our leaders talked.

Later I became a public information staff writer at The Provost Marshal General's School which was the training academy for Military Police officers who were destined for high Army ranks. Although I still disliked the Army, I appreciated the opportunity to write as a way of life. And the work was interesting.

Also, my living arrangement took a turn for the better and my dislike for the Army lessened when, after several months of separation, Mary and our new baby Peggy joined me in Georgia. We lived away from the base in our own apartment in Augusta for the rest of the two-year tour of duty, and that was where I was exposed to the extreme realities of racial segregation.

Getting on a bus one day in 1955, we casually went to the rear, sat down, and unwittingly caused an incident. The black people around us became disturbed, the bus driver stopped the vehicle, and we were asked to move up front. Everyone on the bus seemed to be in favor of the move, so we moved. The rules of segregation were not being challenged at that time by either blacks or whites in Augusta.

We were being challenged financially though, as we tried to live on private's pay, maintained an apartment, and raised a baby in a strange land. But it was far better than living in a barracks, and it was stabilizing to be part of a family again.

One of the interesting features of life in the 95th Military Government Group was the training going on there. The organization was planning to take over a mythical nation in southeast Asia. That mythical nation matched the area on the map that was then known as Indo-China, and later was to become Vietnam. In 1955, this unusual Army unit, the only one of its kind, was planning the future occupation of that nation which we were then beginning to provide with military "advisors."

When our Army service was almost over, on Christmas Eve of 1955, little Peggy, at 15 months, became deathly ill because of the infection of a congenital intestinal malformation called Meckle's Diverticulum. As peritonitis expanded her abdomen to the size of a watermelon and brought Peggy to the verge of death, the surgeon, Dr. Wylie, said her odds for surviving were probably about one in ten thousand. Actually, she was in a coma for several days, but she survived, thanks to dedication by the team of physicians, successful exploratory surgery, and considerable prayer provided by close relatives, dear friends, and strangers.

We learned much about human generosity and love at University Hospital in Augusta, where we lived in our baby's room around the clock for the 30 days she spent there. Years later, my first sale as a writer was a story about that inspiring experience. It was published by *St. Anthony Messenger* in a Christmas issue, and reprinted a while later in a publication called *Family Digest*.

In March 1956, with baby Peggy still recovering from her fight for life, I was honorably discharged from the Army, received a Good Conduct Medal despite my clashes with authority, and was relieved to be returning to civilian life. After spending some months with Mary's folks at their home in Franklin, and in a tiny third floor apartment in Norwood, we finally got ourselves settled in Dedham's veterans housing project.

That fall I returned to Boston College for my senior year, attending college full-time days while working full-time in a book bindery at night. My dean's list grades continued, and in philosophical logic I received 100 percent in the final examination. When I graduated A. B. *cum laude* in June of 1957, I was 22nd in a class of 307. I had achieved my academic goal, and felt balanced in my personal life.

Our marriage was working well, and I was the proud father of little Peggy, plus our second daughter, Karen. I felt good about being the first O'Connell to go beyond high school, looked forward to life as a responsible citizen, and hoped to find a job in the field of journalism.

Feeling the need to continue my liberal arts education, I applied to and was accepted at Boston University's Graduate School of Arts and Sciences, where I studied part-time for four years toward a Master of Arts degree in history while working full-time in the insurance field.

When I received the master's degree from B.U. in 1961, my daughter Amy had been born, and I was feeling fulfilled in my family life and educational achievements. In a burst of upward mobility, we had moved out to the country and built a new home in Franklin, Massachusetts. The American dream was coming together for me, and in a very real sense, the world seemed to be my oyster.

While at Boston College, I had devised a plan for future work. I would not spend more than five years in any given occupation, and would move from one position to another to broaden my life experience. Viewing the world of work as a continuing education process, I felt this approach would permit me to experiment with different ways of life, keep me from getting stale, help me to avoid being trapped by my own career, create challenges for me, and provide a framework for a life based on a broad perspective.

This concept was to be part of my consciousness for many years. During the first annual cycle of activity in a position, I would work out a plan for meeting organizational needs. Then I would refine the approach, achieve what I could for my employer, and begin to think about moving on to something new. There was always an excitement in the thought of moving on, because I have always had a restless creative spirit.

6
Work, Service, Health & Happiness

At age 25, with my degree from Boston College, and the writing experience I had amassed in the Army, I had rapidly learned that the world of journalism was not waiting for me with open arms. Since the only jobs available with newspapers paid less than I needed to support a family, I took a job as an insurance claims investigator with Automobile Mutual Insurance Company of America, ranked by many as the finest company of its kind.

So, on a Friday I left the world of college student and factory laborer, and on the following Monday I was in a suit, with a briefcase and a new company car, joining the executive segment of the workforce. In short order, we were in a position to move from the veterans housing project into our new home in Franklin where we blended with the mainstream of the American middle class.

The main thrust of my position as a claims investigator was to interview people involved in highway accidents, and to a lesser degree, accidents at home. I learned how rapidly one lapse in attention can radically change a person's life. And I learned much about the relativity of truth when it comes to observations people make about their own behavior.

I also enjoyed the freedom that went with the work, since I was on the road most of the time. I roamed freely around the City of Boston as well as neighboring towns, visiting inner city neighborhoods and suburban homes of the affluent. Because I saw people in their homes as well as at their jobs, I observed them in just about every type of work and living situation. This was a wonderful education that is not available to many people.

When 1962 approached, I had been awarded my master's degree, and was nearing my five-year point. So I began to explore employment possibilities in the nonprofit sector. The Massachusetts Safety Council, which is a private, nonprofit, accident prevention organization, responded to my query and created a position for me that would utilize my writing ability. Financially, the work was an exercise in downward mobility because I had to give up a company car. But the work was satisfying to the part of me that wanted to improve the lot of humanity while honing my communication skills.

My initial function at the Safety Council was supervising the fund raising effort, and my challenge was to raise enough money that first year to support the job the Council had created for me. We exceeded the goal, and then I became the Council's public information director. I helped expand the Council's communications through mass media, lectured and broadcasted on accident prevention, and wrote a number of feature articles for magazines. Also, I was a participant in pioneering efforts in highway safety under executive director Bruce Campbell.

Overcoming my fear of public speaking, I served as a legislative spokesperson at hearings during the Council's campaign to win enactment of a bill requiring compulsory seat belt installation in all new cars sold in Massachusetts. This was the kind of activity at the state level that eventually led to seat belts becoming standard equipment in automobiles. There is satisfaction in knowing that countless lives have been saved, and injuries lessened or avoided, due to the pioneering efforts of highway safety crusaders such as the team at the Safety Council.

At the Council, I was named to the Governor's Highway Safety Subcommittee on Education, and I met leaders in government as well as many of the top corporate sector leaders in Boston. Our board of governors was like a *Who's Who* in Massachusetts.

Although the work held a strong interest for me, I was feeling financial pressure due to the Council's conservative pay structure, and I was becoming ambitious to take on higher responsibilities. So I sought new employment in 1964 and competed with about 100 applicants for the position of executive director of the Chevrolet Dealers Association serving dealers in Massachusetts and Rhode Island.

I won the job, and became chief executive of this trade association that provided educational programs and seminars for its members. Once again I was driving a company car, this time a new Chevrolet, and supporting my family became less of a struggle. While learning about the world of franchises, and the inner workings of the automotive industry, I enjoyed the challenge of supervising my own office staff. I worked to expand membership, increased public service activity, wrote newsletters, handled a mass media outreach, and developed legislative information projects.

Feeling the creative urge, I also began writing novels in my spare time. This activity might be described as my passion. It became a combination of obsession and compulsion, and in a very real sense I can look back at those years and say that I was addicted to fiction writing then. It was far more challenging and satisfying than the prose I was creating at work, even though I got satisfaction from the prose too.

Professionally, I became affiliated with the New England Society of Association Executives, and eventually served as a member of the board of directors. At that time I was also a member of the Publicity Club of Boston.

Developing a fascination for politics, I ran for a seat on the Dedham School Committee, and lost the first time I tried. The town moderator appointed me to the Committee to Study Future School Building Needs of the Town of Dedham, and I became the secretary and the public information liaison for the committee. When I ran for office again a year later, I won a seat on the School Committee.

In my second year on the committee, I was named vice chairman by my fellow members. And when 1966 arrived I was named chairman of the committee. I had come from the other side of the tracks next to the East Dedham Railroad station, and had risen to a role of community leader, and was proud of the achievement. At age 34, I was the youngest school board chairman in the history of the community. For me, it was a source of satisfaction to preside at committee meetings, address high school graduating classes, and officiate at various functions.

While serving on Dedham's School Committee, I helped institute the first collective bargaining with teachers, and stimulated high school expansion and junior high renovation. I had the honor of holding the special symbolic shovel at the groundbreaking for the new addition to Dedham High School. I pushed for expansion of the school system's guidance and remedial reading programs. I proposed the development of a school newsletter to inform the community. And I helped increase state and federal funding. I ran for re-election, with no opposition.

When my five-year point with the Chevrolet Dealers Association approached, I believe I was in the early years of what some people describe as a mid-life crisis. I was not satisfied with my direction, even though our family now had a measure of material success and I was attracting some personal recognition.

At this time I was being encouraged by some people to run for office at the state level, but came to the conclusion that it was not the right way of life for me. I wanted time to write novels based on my own experiences in life, and I needed to nourish my writing talent. So, in 1968, at age 36, I resigned from the Dedham School Committee after a year into my second term, and concentrated on my writing.

There's an old saying that life is what happens while you're making other plans. And I can attest to that sentiment. My personal life in the late '60s was very challenging. Mary and I were having marital difficulties, and after one particularly trying evening I ended up screaming and crying uncontrollably, and had an out-of-body experience.

I found myself up above my own body, looking down at my lifeless form on the bed. Staying in that place for a while, somewhere between life and death, I knew I had a choice. I could leave the body then, or return. The key factor in my decision to return was curiosity. I wanted to see what happened with my marriage, my children, my work, and my life. So I returned to the body and continued life with a much freer feeling because I had made the choice to live.

During this period of material success, we bought a second home on Shore Road in Ogunquit, Maine, the area that native Americans had named "Beautiful Place by the Sea." In that setting I wrote fiction and Mary painted portraits. The whole arrangement was almost too good to be true. Even after just a few weeks, that first summer proved to be medicine for the ill health I was experiencing.

From the time of my marriage at age 21 until age 34, my health had been in fairly good balance except for some allergies and difficult bouts with virus infections. But now I was afflicted by irritable bowel syndrome, borderline diabetes, hypertension, and chronic fatigue. The stress of life in 20th Century America had caught up with my sensitive nervous system. And I was paying a price.

On reflection, it's apparent to me that as I had become more successful in the material world, I had also been less spiritually inclined. I even wondered if God had turned his attention to other parts of the universe instead of our planet. I was thinking like an agnostic, but some more bouts with adversity would soon move me into a closer relationship with God.

Our first summer spent in the cottage next to the Museum of Art of Oqunquit was a turning point for us. This brief period away from the stress, tension, and rioting that was taking place in Boston in the late 1960s was all Mary and I needed to convince us to make a move from Dedham to the Maine coast. So we sold our house in Dedham, paid off the mortgage in Maine, and relocated.

Entering my fifth year with the Chevrolet Dealers Association, I proposed another arrangement in which I would become an independent consultant, relocate their office from the South Shore of Massachusetts to the North Shore, and still continue to serve them as a part-time executive director. The board of directors accepted the plan, and I was able to commute to Massachusetts after settling in Maine, with its awe-inspiring coastline and stimulating air.

After our first year of living in Maine, I resigned from the automotive trade association and returned to insurance claims work to support the family while I continued writing my novels. I became the Maine and New Hampshire claims representative for the Crum & Forster Insurance Companies, with an office in Portland, Maine. The job provided a company car, the freedom of only having to spend one day a week at Portland, and a pace that suited my temperament. Also, I had energy and time for other pursuits such as teaching courses in logic and philosophy at New Hampshire College's Portsmouth Center.

While living in Maine I wrote novels, solicited publishers without success, and eventually found a literary agent in New York, Howard Moorepark, who appreciated my work but was unable to sell it for me despite what he called "its merits." The lack of success prodded me to go on writing...and on...and on. But it was depressing to write and not sell. It surely had its impact on my frame of mind. Our marriage was not going well in our new setting, and I was using alcohol and valium to cope with life.

Also, I experienced a shocking setback in my health. One morning I woke up feeling very strange. In the bathroom mirror I saw that my left eye was frozen open and my mouth was distorted. The left side of my face felt the way it feels after having Novocain at the dentist. And I was drooling. It looked as if I had received a stroke. I could neither close my left eye nor use the left side of my mouth. The frightening symptoms lingered for weeks.

Finally, a visit to the Lahey Clinic in Boston brought a verdict of "Bell's Palsy," a condition affecting a cranial nerve. Slowly, my face returned to normal. Although the situation terrified me, it prompted me to write myself an inspirational essay, reflecting on the difficulties of life, expressing my deep belief in God, and accepting everything that had ever happened to me. I was getting close to God again through the adversity that he had provided.

As for our marriage, a shining ray of light came to us on June 20, 1970, when our son Sean was born at nearby Portsmouth Hospital. He was greeted with joy by his three sisters, his mother and me. But, even with the joyful distraction of Sean's presence in our home, our marriage was in the throes of considerable emotional trauma. Without providing details, I can only say that our Maine winters resembled some of the scenes in Tolstoy's *Anna Karenina*. For Mary and I to spend large amounts of time with each other seemed to be toxic to us. Or perhaps I should say we became allergic to each other. Asking God's help, we decided to move back to Massachusetts.

As the job search began, an ad in the Boston Globe attracted my attention. An executive director was needed for Boston's public housing tenants organization, and I knew my years of association management with the Massachusetts Safety Council and Chevrolet Dealers Association would be assets. So I entered competition with about 100 others, and was chosen to be leader and spokesperson for the Boston Public Housing Tenants Policy Council, representing Boston's 55,000 public housing tenants.

I soon learned about the flaws in public housing, sat with the commissioners of the Boston Housing Authority as tenant representative, represented the tenants in battles with City Hall where Mayor Kevin White presided, and I did liaison work with state and federal officials. I was able to help the organization win the campaign to enact a precedent-setting lease and grievance procedure spelling out tenants' rights and the Housing Authority's obligations. To further organizational goals, I waged mass media campaigns to heighten public awareness of conditions in the housing projects. Obviously, my basic love of mass communication moved with me from job to job.

Although I only served with the tenants for less than a year, because their funding had run dry, it was an action-packed time resembling in intensity the months politicians spend leading up to a major election. I met with the mayor privately to sound him out on key issues, arranged forums at City Hall for the tenants, and worked to expand communication with government, the public, and with the members of the tenant organization. As my last official act, I organized a very highly publicized tour of Boston's housing projects by U.S. Senator Edward Brooke.

My next job search took me into competition for the role of executive director of the Massachusetts Federation of Nursing Homes, which happened to be headquartered in my hometown of Dedham. I won the contest, but three months later when the board's second choice visited me, I told him, "When you didn't get this job, you were lucky. The intensity is beyond belief." I believe it was the most stressful and fatiguing three years of my life.

From 1972 to 1975, as the executive director of the trade association representing more than 300 nursing homes in Massachusetts, I helped expand government relations. Also, I organized legislative activity leading to governmental reorganization at the state level. In addition, I coordinated a dynamic campaign to persuade the state to enact a deficiency budget to pay some 70 million dollars in overdue obligations to health care providers in the Bay State. The campaign was successful, and very exhausting.

I also stimulated more educational programs for nursing home personnel, promoted higher ethical standards, developed visibility for the industry in the broadcast media, and created newsletters and Sunday supplements in the Boston newspapers to enhance the image of long-term health care facilities.

Even though I did not love politics, the demands of my post as executive director had transformed me into a political coalition organizer, media campaign tactician, and health care leader. But I was also, once again, pressing my luck with my health, and I began to feel "burned out" physically and emotionally. Along with the intensity of the job, my marital life was steadily deteriorating, and although I continued working on my novels and had various agents representing me, my books were still not selling.

Another problem during this time was that my work in the political arena, based on the art of the possible, raised questions about my own principles and caused dismay. But a business recession was in process, jobs were scarce, and I saw no way out of the situation. On the plus side, I was paid well, and was able to take business-related trips with Mary to beautiful spots like Hawaii and England.

Various pleasures and successes in my life, however, have always carried a price, I have learned. My body and psyche, for example, have been relatively unconcerned with success, and instead have preferred a moderate pace, creative satisfaction, and balance. So, eventually I had to visit my family physician for the verdict: "Nervous exhaustion." My ears felt flushed. My aorta was giving off loud sounds. And to add to my anxieties, a skin cancer developed behind my right ear.

One stress after another built at this time. My uncle was dying of cancer. My wife was getting involved in automobile accidents, and threatening to separate from me. And I was stricken by a viral infection that left me feeling weak from the waist down. It was as if an electrical switch had been thrown, cutting off a vital supply of energy. That feeling of exhaustion haunted me for many years, and at times it could be oppressive.

Suffering from chronic fatigue and ongoing sadness, I nevertheless organized great legislative victories, became a media personality, attracted the recognition of my peers, and served on boards of directors of professional societies. I felt trapped by my own life though. My marriage was becoming less of a marriage. My creative writing goals had not paid off. And I felt that I was not measuring up to my own hopes and dreams when it came to family happiness and personal creativity.

Adversity again proved helpful to me, because in the midst of my suffering I discovered the work of psychologist Carl Jung, and found explanations in his writings that helped me in my own search for meaning in life. I could relate to Jung's thinking, and I credit his work with getting me to see life from a more healthy perspective. It became obvious that I had to change the direction I was following.

So I began looking for a college teaching job after three years of exhausting intensity with the nursing home association. With high level contacts at the State House, I was able to meet influential people, and I explored the possibility of shifting to an academic career. One high ranking educator said to me, "With your vast experience, you are either a candidate for a special award or a heart attack!" It was not my destiny to receive either one. I soon found that full-time teaching openings at the college level were few and far between, and nowhere near the level of pay I needed to meet obligations.

Then, from a friend, I heard about the coming retirement of the current executive director of the Massachusetts Safety Council, where I had served as public information director ten years earlier. When the screening process was over, I had the job, and feeling a bit like Rip Van Winkle, I went back to head up the organization I had left 10 years before.

I was 43 when I was appointed chief executive officer of the Massachusetts Safety Council, Inc., and once again I had the mission of preventing accidents on the highways, in the home, and in the workplace. In a short time, I became recharged with new energy and set ambitious goals for the organization.

To achieve the Council's goals, I attracted new funding for media campaigns on the need to support the 55 mph speed limit, and eventually launched a dynamic highway courtesy campaign which carried the slogan, "A Little Courtesy Won't Kill You."

Due to the nature of the work, I became a highly visible spokesperson in the news and information media, and became a regular guest on major Boston area talk shows and news features. Also, I was featured in many public service commercials.

There was much satisfaction in the position, and it seemed for a while to be the kind of place where I might stay for a long time. I became a member of the Governor's Highway Safety Committee, served on the executive committee of National Safety Council's Conference of State and Local Safety Organizations, and I enjoyed such activities as presenting awards to outstanding citizens. An objective observer might have said I had a lot going for me at the time. I had earned a reputation as a crusader in the public interest, received constant recognition locally, and even gained attention at the national level for the kinds of campaigns I was waging in Massachusetts.

The boy from the wrong side of the tracks had risen to considerable heights. I had my house in the suburbs and my place on the Maine coast. I was a highly visible figure in one of the nation's major metropolitan areas. And I was able to use my intelligence and creativity in useful ways. But still there was something deep down inside that remained uncomfortable with the direction my life was taking.

My exhausted feeling kept returning. Intestinal problems arose. High blood pressure continued. And tears would come into my eyes for no apparent reason. Tranquilizers didn't help. And alcohol was no solution for me because a depressant drug is not an antidote for exhaustion.

Much of the pressure in my life, I am sure, came from within me, based on my inherent existential restlessness. But the marital difficulties continued. And I felt animosity from a faction on my board of directors. I had learned in organizational work that no matter how well conceived your efforts are as a leader, and no matter how effective you are in moving an organization toward its goals, there will always be some people in power on your governing board or executive committee who feel determined to oppose you. Their reasons for this are seldom rational, and can be very irksome.

Behind the scenes at the Safety Council I had some very militant opposition to contend with, and it wore at my patience. I would win battle after battle, but I got tired of needing to fight the battles. And although there was much satisfaction to be gained at the Council, administration of any kind had always gone against my grain. Hiring and firing personnel, and supervising them, was not my cup of tea. I was more of a creative campaigner than an administrator. I thrived on action that brought results.

So, in 1978, after much reflection, and having had a spiritual awakening that I will describe in the next chapter, I decided to leave the Massachusetts Safety Council and build a new organization called the Health Information Institute, Inc. The new entity would have a small board of directors that would not be divided by factions. It would be a not-for-profit corporation. And it would work on critical health issues not being addressed by others.

I put considerable energy into the project, but was unable to attract the needed funding. As I look back, it is obvious that God had other plans than the ones I devised. But I persisted late into 1978, until all of my financial resources had dried up. I was determined not to return to administrative work. And then a twist of fate led me into a reluctant decision to become a communications consultant to health and human service organizations.

A grant I had sought from the Massachusetts Commission for the Blind had come close to being approved, and on the strength of that, a key person there had recommended me to Tufts/New England Medical Center to handle a media project involving a division working with quadriplegics.

With Tufts as my first freelance client, I began soliciting new work, and within six months I had as many clients as I could handle, was earning as much money as I had received at the Safety Council, and had the freedom of managing my own affairs. My work as a mass media campaigner, freelance writer, and editorial consultant led me to one United Way organization after another, and I was able to learn about the inner workings of a wide range of health and human service organizations.

During the late 1970s and the 1980s I worked with hospitals, visiting nurses, addiction treatment centers, educational organizations, lung associations, and family service agencies. For several years I was media consultant to Family Counseling & Guidance Centers which had a network of clinics in Boston and surrounding areas.

Since God works in mysterious and fascinating ways, I also became a communications consultant to the central office of the Catholic Charities serving Greater Boston. Life had taken me from childhood in a Catholic Charities group foster home to consultant for the agency overseeing the Catholic Charities in eastern Massachusetts. Working with the agency's leaders, I kept my secret, and it was heartwarming to learn of their dedication to their clients.

Being an independent consultant has provided me with a continuing education in the world of health and human services, and also has given me many challenges in working with all kinds of people trying to serve others. The work has had its ups and downs, but there is always a price for freedom. And the freedom to serve others as a specialist, not as an administrator, has been worth the price.

I have come to realize that working as a freelance consultant in modern America has much in common with the role of fishermen in the time of Jesus. One's way of life is not secure, not fixed. One is not in control. One is subject to forces which cannot be rationally understood. And one has to constantly remind oneself that the will of God must prevail, whether things are on the upswing to prosperity or on the way down into financial distress.

My life as a freelance writer motivated me to become a member of the American Medical Writers Association, and eventually I was elected president of the New England Chapter, and served on the board of directors of the national organization. I have also attended AMWA conferences in various U.S. and Canadian cities. In Toronto a few years ago, I presented a session titled "Launching a Freelance Writing Career." Later I was asked to write a chapter on that subject for the AMWA book, *Biomedical Communication*.

Life as a freelancer has been fascinating. From 1979 to 1981 I had my own TV public affairs show on Boston's Channel 25, which was then owned by the Christian Broadcasting Network. I conceived and hosted "It's Your Life," which ran for nearly three years. Tim Robertson, son of Pat Robertson of CBN, directed the show for me. On my show I interviewed community leaders, and spiritual leaders such as David DuPlessis, who was called "Mister Pentecost;" Chaplain Ray, who did a prison ministry; and other dedicated Christians who carried the message of God's love. During those years I came to respect and love a large number of evangelical Christians who really meant it when they encouraged one another and said, "Praise the Lord."

As my work led me to agencies dealing with the addictions, I began to specialize in addiction writing.

Addiction is our world's major health problem, and our most serious spiritual problem, since addictions are the idols that get between us and our Creator. In 1983 I became a national correspondent for the *U.S. Journal of Drug and Alcohol Dependence*, and served in this capacity for eight years during which I attended conferences on addiction, listened to the experts, interviewed them, and wrote feature articles to inform health professionals.

I also wrote for publications such as *The Journal* of the Addiction Research Foundation in Toronto and the *Medical Post*, a Canadian publication. In *Catholic Digest*, I wrote feature stories about the life of Boston's Cardinal Medeiros and about the "Junkie Priest," Father Dan Egan, whom I interviewed at the Graymoor monastery in New York.

Also, working in the addiction field led me to take a look at my own use of alcohol and valium, and in 1983 I decided to abstain from alcohol and other chemicals. The decision was a healthy one, and since that time I have not found it necessary to consume mind altering substances. That has left my mind free for God to do the altering.

Before I leave this part of the writing, which brings us into the 1980s in my work life, I want to note that my marriage of 27 years ended early in 1981. Instead of growing together, we had grown apart, and developed differences that could not be reconciled. Our separation led to divorce, loneliness, adjustment to solitary living, and growth of new self-esteem based on love of self and others.

At the time of the separation, my three daughters were young adults, but my son was only 10, and it was difficult to no longer live with him. The early months of separation from him and my home were lonely beyond description. However, we spent quality time together as the years passed, developed a very consistent relationship, and became friends as well as father and son. The pain of divorce seemed almost unbearable at times, but we lived through it, and grew emotionally. For me, the idea of divorce had been unthinkable, but apparently it was necessary for me to experience it, as many others have had to.

Every portion of my life has been part of a mosaic, often misunderstood by me, but important in God's master plan for my spiritual development. In this process, I have played opposite parts a number of times. I have been a married man and a divorced person, factory worker and high executive, subordinate and leader, voter and elected official, student and teacher, poor and well off, renter and property owner, participant in accidents and accident prevention leader, a person terrified of speaking in public and a professional lecturer, a talk show guest and later a talk show host, borderline agnostic and enthusiastic believer. I have had a vast and varied set of experiences during this time on earth that we call life. And I have had many dreams come true.

As I look back on my life, I can see that it was necessary for me to spend long periods of time alone during those important years that eventually led to my spiritual enlightenment at Peterborough in the Monadnock Mountains on September 5, 1985. In spiritual development, the ability to endure and then enjoy solitude is part of the process. Surely the years of prayer and meditation in solitude helped prepare me for the upward climb in those special mountains.

7
Spiritual Training

The fall of 1977 was a key time in my spiritual adventure, and I was reading heavily in the works of Carl Jung. A few doors down Beacon Street from my Safety Council office on Beacon Hill, where I had a view of the golden dome of the State House, there was a fine private library with a complete collection of Jung's works. It is called the Athenaeum, and I spent many lunch periods there. Also, at home I immersed myself in my own copy of the Jung book that fascinated me most: *Mysterium Coniunctionis*, which in Latin means Mystery of the Conjunction.

Jung was a guiding spirit for me during that time of working toward wholeness, and I gathered vital insights from his exploration of symbolism and the world of the unconscious mind. Although we can't substitute book learning for experience, my life has been strongly influenced by psychological, mystical, and spiritual reading which has often enhanced my existence and has given me much inspiration.

During the 1970s, I developed deep respect for Jung's work, and I read extensively in the writings of Thomas Merton, C.S. Lewis, Albert Camus, Thomas a Kempis, and Erich Fromm, among others. But in the end, I have to say that the real test of spiritual growth has been daily living, and learning to relate well to self, others, and God.

Even Jung, a prolific writer and insatiable reader, had this to say on the subject: "Put away your academic gown. Say good-bye to the study and wander with the human heart through the world. There, in the horror of the prison, the asylum, and the hospital, in the drinking shops, brothels, and gambling halls, in the salons of the elegant, in the exchanges, socialist meetings, churches, religious revivals, the sectarian ecstasies, through love and hate, through the experience of passion in every form in your own body you would reap richer stores of knowledge than textbooks a foot thick could give you. Then would you know how to doctor the sick with real knowledge of the human soul."

The more I absorbed Jung's work, the more I grappled with my own spiritual condition. And in the fall of 1977 I came across a reference to the Book of Job in his writing. It motivated me one evening to reach up to the bookcase behind my bed and take down my Bible, which was just like new because it was one of the least read books in my collection. I hadn't taken it seriously since using it in a theology class at Boston College in the early 1950s.

As I read about Job's life, I could relate to much that was written there. Job's situations were different, but I could identify with his losses. I reflected on my painful years of marital deterioration, my chronic fatigue, the burnout I felt from work situations, and my questioning of the very meaning of life itself. In the Book of Job I saw how a relatively innocent, basically moral man, who tended to be complacent and a bit self-righteous, could be allowed by God to suffer intensely in order to gain deeper insights into the God/man relationship.

My study of the Book of Job led to more frequent Bible reading. Then late on the evening of November 20, 1977, I took the Bible, which had been part of my library but not an integral part of my life, and I dropped it onto my lap as I lay there on the bed, propped up with my pillow. Without me having any conscious part in the process, the book of 1600 pages fell open to John 20-21.

I looked at the pages casually, and then I was startled to see my own name there. Thomas. What an interesting coincidence, I thought, that the Bible should open to a section about Thomas, the doubter. I began reading about the resurrection of Jesus, his visit to see his disciples, and Thomas's doubt which was followed by renewed faith, and Jesus's repeated appearances to his followers after death.

Something unexpected happened to me as I read "Feed my lambs," "Feed my sheep," and "Follow me." Tears began streaming down my cheeks, and I started to tremble with excitement. Then I felt the presence of Jesus in my room, and his picture on the wall above my typewriter developed a whole new aura. As the reality of Jesus touched my heart, that picture came alive in a multi-dimensional way. And as I write this, many years later, tears are once again filling my eyes. Tears of gratitude and wonder. What a turning point that evening was for me!

I slid from my bed, and went to my knees on the floor, with tears still streaming down my face, and I asked Jesus to forgive me for doubting his reality. I asked him to take over my life, and I thanked him for coming to me through his words in my Bible. I told him how grateful I was that, in a way I could not hope to understand, he had opened my mind and heart to him. From that evening on I was a new spirit, a new being. I had been born again.

That experience led me into an ongoing practice of Bible reading, usually late in the evening, and nearly always in a "random selection" way, closing my eyes and inserting a fingernail into a page at random, and then absorbing the material on the two pages facing me, plus the material on the preceding and following pages, with special attention to the first words my eyes would see on opening the book.

God's Word continued to come alive for me, as day by day I dipped into the Spirit of the Scriptures and always saw words I could link to my daily life. During the first two weeks of intentional random selection, the passages John 20-21 came to me on two other occasions, against great odds. But in the realm of God there are no odds, there are just wonders unfolding that go beyond the boundaries of our limited minds.

Early in the process, I began noting the dates of my random Bible reading in the margins of my text, and over time trends would develop on subjects important to me. So I came to believe that God, who is unlimited, can communicate to us directly through his Word. From November 1977 to June 1978 I compiled enough information on my communication with God to fill a book 200 pages long. But here I can only touch on a few of the mystical events of that precious time.

For example, a number of spiritual messages came to me at the Athenaeum, and one was in a book by Simone Weil that I picked up casually. In *Intimations of Christianity Among the Ancient Greeks*, these words leaped out at me: "One must renounce in favor of God, through love for him and for the truth, this illusory power which he has accorded us to think in the first person...the renunciation of the power to think in the first person is the abandonment of all worldly goods in order to follow the Christ." It was difficult at that time for me to envision doing what those words suggested, but time has verified her words for me, and I have been led into the path she described.

Looking into God's word for guidance, I made the decision to leave my post at the Massachusetts Safety Council. I offered six months notice so I would be on hand to launch the highway courtesy campaign I had conceived, and my resignation was accepted on that basis. Then I began formulating some plans for developing a new nonprofit agency called the Health Information Institute, Inc.

During the early part of 1978 I had a vivid dream that may have predicted my visit to the mountains in September 5, 1985, about seven years into the future, and may have a bearing on future events on the planet. Here is what I saw in the twilight state between waking and sleeping: Blazing fire lit up the sky as I saw two huge mountains with a valley in between. Then, behind the mountains, I saw a large portion of the sky glowing with a light beyond description, in contrast with the dark outlines of the two mountains.

Then the mountain was pulling me onward, beckoning me to climb the mountain to see what was on the other side in the glow of the bright light. "Come! Come through the fire...and on into the light! Come!" The next day I submitted my written resignation to the Safety Council. And I moved on into the unknown set of adventures that would eventually lead me to the Monadnock Mountains to experience God's power in a personal way.

God's power became evident to me again a few weeks later, during the blizzard of 1978. On the evening of February 7, in the middle of the storm, I drifted into the twilight zone between waking and sleeping, and a voice said to me: "...everything will be fading into one. It will take about 50 years for this to happen, but it will happen." My immediate intuition, when I came back to full consciousness with a start, was that the world as we know it would end in about 50 years when Jesus returns for his 1,000 year reign. It would become a unified world.

As the years unfolded, and I worked with health and human service agencies as a communications consultant, my daily mystical adventure continued unabated. For example, I experienced three dramatic visions of Jesus Christ. On two occasions, when I was in the mysterious twilight zone between waking and sleeping, a full-sized, very rugged looking Jesus appeared and stood at the foot of my bed, silently. Jesus's appearance in those visions was very similar to the image on the Shroud of Turin.

Around this time, thinking how different Jesus looked in my vision compared to glorified portraits of him, I whispered to the picture of Jesus in my room, "You looked so different in my visions of you." To my amazement, Jesus's voice came into my mind and said, "What did you expect me to look like after all I went through?"

On another occasion, after my marital separation, when I was living in Canton, Massachusetts, in the early 1980s, there was a ferocious lightning storm one evening, and on my window shade several trees outside cast shadows that took on the form of Jesus for several minutes. The next morning I saw that a large tool shed had been lifted over a high fence and demolished by the strong winds. What power!

The early months of my marital separation, in February 1981, were a time of grief, emotional pain, and deep loneliness, but also provided a continuing succession of spiritual experiences. Lost in the sea of my own solitude, I immersed myself in the Bible, and one night as I read about him being scourged and ridiculed and spat upon by angry men, I cried until I was exhausted and shouted, "Oh, Jesus! What you suffered to show God's love for us!" I asked him to keep me from feeling sorry for myself even though I felt so alone and misunderstood.

During that lonely time that I thought of as my own forty days and nights in the desert, I spent many hours reading *The Cloud of Unknowing*, meditating on it night after night. That book led me to a more consistent approach to silent, sitting meditation. I had some unlearning to do, some unknowing to accomplish, and also needed some major healing for my wounded spirit.

After wandering around in a semi-daze for about ten months, and questioning my own identity as I moved away from 27 years of marriage, I was led by a friend to a support group organized by the Friars of the Atonement for separated and divorced Christians in the chapel at Westgate Mall in Brockton.

In that little chapel, I had my first experience of group therapy, and learned to share my feelings of fear, doubt, and insecurity. I joined a small group there called the Self Awareness Program (SAP), where I grew emotionally and spiritually, along with other kindred spirits. Rev. Hindemuth, a Lutheran minister, guided us away from the blame-the-former-spouse game and into a period of vital personal growth. This experience of the healing power of the group led me to explore Twelve Step recovery groups as the years went by, and they are now an important part of my life. Twelve Step groups are my safe harbor regardless of how stormy life may be.

With my friends from the chapel, I attended a retreat for separated and divorced Christians at Graymoor in New York, during September 1983. In one of my random Bible readings at Graymoor, the words of Joshua 1 said this to me: "As long as you live, no one shall be able to stand in your way. I will be with you as I was with Moses. I will not leave you or desert you. Be strong and stand firm." Ephesians 4 said to me, "You must put aside your old self, which gets corrupted by illusory desires. Your mind must be renewed by a spiritual revolution."

Everyone else who went with me on the retreat was housed in the new wing of the monastery. But I was led to the old building, with its small monastic cells. The water in the showers was cold there, if you were impatient, and I was impatient as I waited for warm water to come. When I reflected later on the spiritual challenge of developing more patience, I wrote in my journal, "The secret is that there is no secret. It's just hard work."

Coincidentally, my cell was near the cell of a priest named Father Dan Egan, a name I recognized. My client Bill McCue, the executive director of the Third Nail Drug Program in Boston, had told me about "The Junkie Priest." So I introduced myself to him, and asked for an interview while I was on the retreat. Later I wrote an article about him that was published in *Catholic Digest*.

Another incident at the monastery happened when I was praying at the altar in the chapel. There was a representation of Francis of Assisi and the stigmata there. It caught my attention, and gave me a mysterious message I did not understand. This was two years before I experienced my own symbolic wounding in the Monadnock Mountains.

In 1983 I was taking meditation more seriously than ever before, and becoming more disciplined about daily practice. I sat in the ancient silent and motionless way, once a day, every day, no matter how I felt. Then, at a retreat on the Jungian healing archetype at The Common, a Carmelite monastery in Peterborough, New Hampshire, I met people from Massachusetts who meditated together on Thursday evenings. They invited me to join them some time.

A few months later I became part of the group organized by Andy and Marie Foley in Brookline. Then I committed to meditating not once but twice a day, for at least 20 minutes and averaging about 30 minutes. The tradition was based on the work of Father John Main, trained in meditation in India. He had spread the word about it in England and at the Benedictine monastery in Montreal.

At first I sat in a chair, and eventually moved to a Zen pillow with legs crossed on the floor. This practice was to become the top priority in my life, and has remained so. I believe it helps us burn up old karmic debts, and apparently I had much to burn up.

So, with a new commitment to meditation giving me a spiritual foundation as 1984 opened, I was led into a still more intensive series of experiences that I now believe were all designed to prepare me for that special day that was to come in September 1985.

One chain of events was set in motion by Mark Keller, a pioneer in the alcoholism field. While I was interviewing him for a story I was writing for the *U.S. Journal of Drug and Alcohol Dependence*, he said he was going to present a lecture at a conference in Israel during September 1984. Then he gave me a copy of the program for Israel's first International Congress on Alcohol Dependence, the Family, and the Community. "You should go there," he said.

When I told Mark I didn't have the money for the trip, he simply said, "Find a way." There was something about his attitude that reached a deep place in me, and so I began to explore options. One of them turned out to be the sale of my last piece of personal real estate, a condo in New Hampshire's White Mountains, near Intervale.

Before my divorce, I had owned my own home in Dedham, a second home on the Maine coast with no mortgage, and a half interest in a rundown tenement my uncle Joe had left me. Divorce led me to sign over my share of my former home to Mary so my son Sean would have security about housing. The house in Maine was sold to pay debts and taxes. And the tenement was a white elephant. Its value was eroded by lawyers' fees in a complicated litigation. So all I had left was the small condo in North Conway, which I had bought with my portion from the sale of the Maine cottage. By selling the condo I secured my plane fare and basic expenses for the Israel trip. And I was now without property.

I also offset some of the costs by convincing three publications to buy stories I would write there: *The U.S. Journal, The Journal* of the Addiction Research Foundation in Toronto, and *Alcoholism Magazine*.

Figuring that this trip to the Middle East might be the only one I would ever take, I added a few days in Rome prior to the conference, and a few days in Egypt later. Without conscious planning, I was arranging a 14-day trip back through ancient times that would help me pull together some of my own spiritual puzzle.

The theme that repeated itself on this pilgrimage was that we are truly one world, and we are all in this adventure of life together. I was fascinated by the ancient burial places in Rome known as the catacombs, and I had similar feelings in Lazarus's tomb in Israel, as well as in the Great Pyramid. I felt the unity of existence when I gazed at Greek and Egyptian art treasures in the Vatican Museum. And I felt the reality of one world in Jerusalem where Arabs function side by side with Israelis.

The Dead Sea Scrolls intrigued me, and I felt awe when I visited the Fifth Station of the Way of the Cross, where Simon had helped Jesus. It was a profound experience to enter the tomb of Lazarus at Bethany. And I meditated in awe near the Garden of Gethsemane at the rock where Jesus had meditated. At Golgotha, near where Jesus was crucified, the shape of a skull could be seen in the rock face, and I had powerful feelings in the Garden Tomb where it is believed Jesus was buried. In a deep way, Jesus became more and more real to me in Jerusalem.

Something else became real to me in Jerusalem, and I did not know how serious it could be. I began to feel weak, sweated a literal flood at night, and started having diarrhea that could not be stopped. It followed me to Egypt, where I was losing two to three pounds a day. Almost in a trance state due to the sweltering heat and the illness, I began to have a kind of mental dyslexia, with words jumbling up in my brain in odd ways. Finally, I found a physician. I was diagnosed as having a severe case of amoebic dysentery, but by God's grace I received excellent medical care that slowly helped me to recover.

In spite of the dysentery, I was only held back from a few of the experiences I thought I would pursue. One place I missed was Luxor. Apparently, it was not necessary for me to go there. Instead, I followed my intuition which led me to the Cairo Museum where I had an affinity for various objects. One of them was a black basalt figure of Horus, the Falcon God, dating to the 27th century B.C. Later, I also picked out two souvenirs at random in a papyrus shop near the pyramids. One was an ankh, which is the Egyptian symbol of life. The other, I learned much later, was a replica of Horus.

To add a note of mystical intrigue to the Horus connection, just as I was leaving the area near the Sphinx a young girl ran up to me with a canvas shopping bag, asked me to buy it, and due to her persistence I bought it. Several months later, a friend pointed to a figure on the bag hanging as a souvenir on my wall, and said, "Horus." I had been wondering about the meaning of Horus since my trip but hadn't realized that the image of Horus was right there in the most obvious place of all, on the shopping bag.

In the Museum at Cairo, I also had strange and powerful feelings in Ikhnaton's room with its statues that seemed like caricatures. Although I am thin, my own shape is similar to his, with a waist that seems large for the body style. Ikhnaton was the heretic king of Egypt who believed in one loving Father God who presided with kindness over our planet.

At Gizeh, in the Great Pyramid, being led toward the central chamber by an Arab with a candle, I came up against a psychic or spiritual wall of energy that warned me to go no further. So, to my guide's dismay, we had to return to the exit. It was not claustrophobia. I felt an ominous and oppressive invisible field. As I stepped out of the tunnel into the light I was relieved to be in dazzling solar brilliance.

Later that year, at Curry College near Boston, during an informal meeting of people interested in Jung's work, an analyst listened to my story about the energy field in the Great Pyramid that operated as a barrier to keep me away from the central chamber.

He said intuitively, "Apparently the person from the East was not the right person to lead you into the inner chamber." He compared the pyramid's inner chamber to my own inner chamber and said, "Maybe yours is a New World destiny, and you are meant to explore your own inner chamber with a guide from the West." Nearly one year later, after exploring various parts of my inner being in the Monadnock Mountains, I remembered his words vividly.

As 1984 closed, I was reading the Egyptian Book of the Dead one evening, and in that twilight state of tiredness where resistance is lowered, I heard one succinct line: "You still don't trust me." So as 1985 opened I decided to try to trust the unknown part of me that seemed to have a clear channel to God.

The months ahead were loaded with symbolic events. Too many to list here. But one stands out. In January I had a dream about a key. Within two days, at the Boston Athenaeum, I was reading Jung's *Aion*, and there I saw a lion-headed figure holding a key in each hand. On that same day, I came across a book for sale at the Dedham Public Library. Its title? *The Key*. A section of the book leaped out at me: "He'd find a door it would open. A special place. No matter how long it took, he'd find the right door." One day later, at a Chinese restaurant, I saw a lion's head almost identical to the one in Jung's *Aion*.

Meaningful coincidences became a way of life for me, and it seemed as 1985 opened that I was moving upward in a spiral of experiences that had started with wide circles at the base, but was intensifying into smaller, more rapid circles as this spiral of energy was moving me toward a point that would culminate in the Monadnock Mountains.

I recall how eye surgery led me to a specialist whose office happened to be next to the C.G. Jung Institute in Boston. After learning that I had to have a triangular, pyramid-shaped growth removed from the white of my right eye, I stopped at the Jung Institute and became interested in a seminar in Egyptian mythology that was scheduled.

The eye surgery exposed me to an electron microscope that sent painfully bright rays into my eye. On the day after the surgery, on the way to the doctor for a checkup, I found a very special book at Horai-san bookstore in Brookline Village: *Studies in Alchemy: Science of Self-Transformation*. While recovering from surgery, I read in this book authored by Mark Prophet/Saint Germain, fascinating insights about the Christ, light, and energy flow; about how splinters of light rays connect with energy sources; and about light as the key to alchemy. I also read about mantras, balance, and unity.

Then, while taking a course at Curry College in Jungian psychology to see if I had interpreted Jung's work correctly, professor Fran McPherson, a mystic, handed me a book she thought I'd enjoy: *A Dossier on the Ascension* by Mark Prophet/Serapis Bey. On the cover was a pyramid. Inside the pyramid an ascension ceremony was shown.

I read at random: "The flame of the ascension is the KEY which unlocks the door to immortality for every man." I also read about the white light of Christ; the White Brotherhood of the light, not a racial term; and about raising "vital energies of sympathetic and central nervous system around the spinal column...to the spiritual eye of perception."

Skeptically, I learned about achieving a lighter physical form when 51 percent of one's karma is balanced and one may be a candidate for ascension. Then, before the seminar at the Jung Institute on February 7, I had one of the most symbolic dreams I have ever experienced. I saw two distinct blue eyes, disembodied, functioning in space, gazing directly at me, and accompanied by the word "commitment." I learned later that in the process of resurrection, eyes of any color may become a beautiful electric blue.

At the Egyptian mythology seminar, the healing eye of Horus was discussed. Then, during a session on symbols, a sheet was passed around, and on it I saw an outline of two eyes very similar to the blue eyes I had dreamed about. At this time, I seemed to be drifting along a river of symbolism to do with eyes and pyramids. On the day after the seminar I flipped open Webster's Reference Library and there I saw the reverse side of the Great Seal of the United States, with its pyramid and all-seeing eye of God.

Around the same time, at the Athenaeum, I read about the Horus myth: "Horus gave his eye to restore the light of day. Horus plays the role of savior." In Jung I learned that "Horus leads directly to Christ." Horus was described as "the rising God."

Daily I learned about Horus, eye symbolism, and pyramid mysteries. And I could see that everything in life is symbolic, no matter how we sense it. Words, for example, are merely symbols of ideas. I did not know it then, but now I see that everything I was learning was part of a spiritual training program designed to teach me that what we see is a kind of illusion, and true reality is based on the invisible.

As my insights deepened, I got in touch with the depths of my own being. And this process was intensified by a June trip to Scotland and Ireland. The trip's purpose was to attend a conference on addiction in the workplace, at the University of Stirling in Scotland. It was sponsored by North Conway Institute, a Boston-based interfaith group founded by Rev. David A. Works and dedicated to providing education on the addictions.

The trip to Ireland was a side trip to explore my Irish roots. I visited the village of Castle Cove which was near Cahirdaniel in County Kerry, where my grandmother Johanna Galvin had spent her early years. Also, my grandfather Dan O'Connell's people had come from the same area, so I visited the nearby home of Daniel O'Connell, an advocate of religious freedom who was to Ireland what Gandhi was to India. Dublin's main street is O'Connell Street!

Having been prepared for the trip to Ireland by hundreds of stories that I had heard from Granny O'Connell, I thoroughly enjoyed the few days I spent there, absorbing the hospitality of the people and the beauty of this mystical isle of sea mist and rainbows.

When I got home, August was approaching, and I didn't think I could spare the time for the annual Cape Cod Writers' Conference at Craigville. I almost decided not to go, but unseen forces moved me to attend from Sunday through Wednesday, leaving myself part of the week for my consulting business. I didn't know that at the conference I was destined to meet someone who would lead me to the Monadnock Mountains where my entire life would be changed.

As the conference opened, an attractive woman caught my eye, and something inside told me to get to know her. The next day I obeyed the inner voice, and introduced myself. We hit it off, and soon I was sharing much of the conference with my new friend Gloria. We talked about many things, including the reality of auras. Gazing at my head, she said she saw a light blue aura, and reported that radiating from my hands she saw the color green, a healing color.

Gloria talked about a New Hampshire mystic and healer named Eleanor Moore. She was vague about what went on in the farmhouse at Peterborough, but she suddenly said to me, "When you go there...." Her confidence that I would visit her was contagious. And immediately I said, "I guess I'm ready for her."

Without delay I called Eleanor Moore, curious to see what she could provide in the way of psychic or mystical insights. We connected, and she had a two-hour space available. So I marked my calendar for 3:00 p.m., Thursday, September 5, 1985.

Shortly before going to New Hampshire, I visited Gloria on Cape Cod. At the end of our visit late in the evening she showed me the aura where trees meet the sky, and pointed to a valley formed by the tops of the trees. I saw a solitary, very bright star, toward the north, and I knew I'd follow that star to New Hampshire. As I drove away from Gloria's house a car cut in front of me. Its registration plate said "ASTRAL." I didn't know the full meaning that night, but at Peterborough the message on that plate would be mentioned by the voice of God.

Now it is clear to me that the license plate with "ASTRAL" on it, and so many other coincidences in my life, were used by God to prepare me for the event I was to experience on September 5. But as I got ready to go to Peterborough, I had no idea what would happen there, except that I knew I would see an interesting mystic in the Monadnock Mountains.

8
Approaching the Mountains

On the morning of September 5, 1985, just before leaving for New Hampshire, I flipped the Bible open at random, and in Chapter 9 of Deuteronomy these words leaped out at me: "Thou shalt know therefore this day that the Lord thy God himself will pass over thee, a devouring and consuming fire...that the Lord may accomplish his word which he promises by oath to thy fathers, Abraham, Isaac, and Jacob." Later that day I would know what the consuming fire was, but when I read those words I had no idea.

One day before my trip, I had made a decision to move to Cape Cod shortly, and on the morning of September 5, as I read Chapter 8 of Deuteronomy, I saw these words: "The Lord thy God will bring thee into a good land...." It was a favorable omen. In *Daily Word*, a Unity booklet, I also read, "My mind and body are radiant with God's perfection and vitality." I learned the meaning of radiance that day.

Driving along Route 128 from Dedham toward Peterborough, I recalled meeting with Gloria at the writers' conference and telling her of my random Bible reading. After she asked me to demonstrate with a small book, I had flipped it open to these words: "Follow your star with confidence." Later, during my visit to see Gloria, she had pointed to the solitary star in the northern sky. And here I was, following that star with confidence.

Gloria had also given me some audio tapes by the entity Ramtha. Before going to see Eleanor Moore I had been playing those tapes. Ramtha said we should love ourselves because self in the purest form is God. And to love self, we should cease to divide it. The kingdom of heaven is within us and puts us into contact with the Father, he said, and talked of a divine fire altering the ego.

He told of Jesus's training by great masters, his confrontation with self in the wilderness, his purging all desire except to achieve the will of the Father, his victory over death, and his demonstration of God's will openly and fearlessly. Ramtha quoted Jesus: "The kingdom of heaven is within you." "The Father and I are one." "You are also Sons of God." These thoughts were present in my mind as I drove.

I brought a manila folder with me, with items to discuss with Eleanor: Meditation. Rome, Jerusalem, and Cairo. Ikhnaton. Horus. Random Bible reading. Various symbols. C.G. Jung. Psychoanalysis. Books. Moving to Cape Cod. Dreams. And other things. In the folder I had a note reminding me to ask about a command I had received in a dream/vision: "The

Work comes first, everything else second." To me, "The Work" meant my spiritual quest, including the work of daily meditation. But I wanted her opinion.

I also brought a description of my only previous experience with a psychic, on March 16, 1977. The information had been misplaced for several years, and a few weeks before my visit to Eleanor, while searching for old notes on dreams, out had fallen the sheet about psychic Pat Harmon-Smith, who had followed me as a guest on a radio show on Boston's North Shore. I was talking about highway safety, and had been asked to stay and let her work on me.

Pat noted my "good lights," "high intelligence bordering on genius," and being ahead of my time with visions and insights. She urged me to hold fast to my ideas and said I was working on a secret project, which was true. She said that in the future I would be inundated with paper work. She was right! And she said there would be a Florida or Caribbean influence in my life. In 1983 I became a national correspondent for the U.S. Journal of Drug and Alcohol Dependence, a journal located in Florida.

As I drove toward New Hampshire, as I prayed to be shown the right path in life, a car pulled in front of me with this plate: "GO." I had recently read in the Scriptures about God answering Moses that way. On the highway, for a while I had a motorcycle escort, with one bike ahead of me and one behind, and this felt odd. Was it a sign that I was being protected on my way to the mountains?

Another experience happened when I stopped for lunch. From a pile of reading material on my back seat I grabbed a book. It was Thomas Merton's *The New Man*. As I waited for my fish and chips, I

decided to open Merton's book at random, and it fell
to pages 122 and 123. My eyes went to section 77.
And I knew the number 7 had divine implications. It
also means completeness, synthesis, and safety. In
Buddhism it signifies the "ascent."

I read this in section 77: "He that is of God hears
the words of God. To be aware of God is to enter into
contact with One, Who, infinitely hidden and
transcendent, cannot be known as He is in Himself
unless He reveals Himself to us." Flipping to the
previous page, 120, and then to page 124, I read:
"Since we are made in the image and likeness of
God, there is no other way for us to find out who we
are than by finding in ourselves the divine image."

Merton wrote, "The recognition of our true self,
in the divine image, is then a recognition of the fact
that we are known and loved by God....In order to
make this leap out of ourselves we have to be willing
to let go of everything that is our own....That does
not mean that we give up thinking and acting; but
that we are ready for any change that God's action
may make in our lives." These words would have an
important meaning late that very afternoon.

Before leaving the restaurant I read the rest of the
chapter titled "Spirit in Bondage," and I underscored
these words: "We must cast away the 'aprons of
leaves' and the 'garments of skins' which the Fathers
of the Church variously interpret as passions, and
attachments to earthly things, and fixation in our
own rigid determination to be someone other than
our true selves." Then, at the bottom of the page I
scribbled, "Key--Journey to Self."

As I drove toward the Monadnock Mountains, I
had no idea that I was going to receive the gift of

direct conscious communication with my Creator. If anyone had told me at that time that I would soon have God's voice blend with mine in a series of messages based on his eternal Love, I would have reacted with complete disbelief. But at Monadnock my belief system was radically altered.

On my trip I missed a major turn and got lost, but eventually found myself entering the familiar village of Peterborough, which was used as the setting for Thornton Wilder's classic, *Our Town*. As I drove into unfamiliar territory, the road got steeper. I was ascending a portion of the Monadnock range.

When I got home later that evening, I checked "monadnock" in Webster's Collegiate Dictionary. The word means a "hill or mountain of resistant rock." Resistance is a factor in electricity, and relates to reluctance. I had often been spiritually reluctant. A "monad" is a "unit, an individual, an atom....It is an individual elementary being, psychical or spiritual in nature, reflecting within itself the whole universe." Monadism is a theory that the universe is comprised of monads. It's like William Blake saying the world can be found "in a grain of sand."

Approaching a fork in the road as I ascended this part of the Monadnock Mountains, I wondered if I had strayed again. Have I gone too far? Am I lost? Do I bear left now? I'm running late!

It was a bit after 3:00 p.m. when I arrived at the yellow farmhouse. The side door was open, so I went in and found women talking in the living room. Asking for Eleanor, I learned she was still with a client and would be available soon. So I sat and waited for the most important meeting in my life.

9
The Monadnock Revelations

I clearly recall the aura of warmth and calmness that radiated from Eleanor Moore as she entered my life with her ready smile and her mild voice. This woman in her sixties, with her graying hair and a bit of extra weight, made me feel very welcome.

After introducing me to her relatives, she invited me into a room with a padded table similar to those used by chiropractors. Then we sat and I told her about how Gloria had referred me to her, my plan to move to Cape Cod shortly, the losses during my early years, my nine years in the group foster home, and the family secret about my mother's insanity.

Early in the visit, Eleanor said Cape Cod would suit me well. Then she reported an Atlantis influence in my life from a previous time. She also said that even though my mother had only been with me a short while, she had still loved me. Eleanor had a very soothing manner.

As the healing session opened, she asked me to remove my sneakers and all metal objects, telling me to place my things on a table. So I took off my watch, belt, and the silver necklace with the bronze crucifix on it. And I removed coins from my pockets. Also, I took the manila folder holding information to discuss with her, and I put it on the table where it was going to stay. I was not in control here, as I was when conducting an interview. This was Eleanor Moore's domain.

As she directed me to lie down on my back on her table, I noticed a picture of C.G. Jung, and told her of my many years of concentration on his work.

We discussed synchronicity, and such meaningful coincidences as the way my meeting with Gloria had led to my trip to Peterborough to see Eleanor. As I relaxed on her table, she encouraged me to talk about my spiritual journey. So I told her of my random selection Bible reading, and she said, "That's the only way to read." I shared the details of my trip to the Middle East. And when I reviewed the decline and fall of my nearly thirty-year marriage, Eleanor said Mary and I had not been right for each other due to childhood trauma and astrological differences.

Soon I was telling her about the most intimate concerns of my life, including the confusion of being single after so many years of marriage, and she said I would find a woman who needed someone like me. Then she grinned and said, "I could go for you myself, but I'm quite a bit older than you."

We talked about my meditation practice, and as we talked she began to touch me very lightly in various places, rubbing my feet and other body parts softly. She mentioned "blocks" that existed in the body due to past emotional trauma, and explained that they were part of the body's energy system, and were barriers I had not been able to break through by myself, despite my meditation discipline.

During that first hour, I vented much that had frustrated or harmed me, and I felt tingling in my feet. She said, "That's good." Then came twitches throughout my body, the type of muscular twitches I had felt throughout my life. But now I got a flood of them. She said it meant healing was taking place, and "tight tension" was being released.

As she continued to move around, touching me lightly, the twitching escalated, and the tingling in my feet spread through my body. Soon my intestines, especially the colon, began leaping in a strange way. I had suffered from "irritable bowel" periodically, so the healing had found the right target.

The tingling I felt wasn't the prickly "pins and needles" sensation. It was like the tingling felt along with a burst of fear or embarrassment, or seeing blood. As the tingling built, I was sharing the truths of my life with Eleanor, holding nothing back. She encouraged and soothed me, and while I talked tears flowed from my eyes in a steady stream.

Personal disclosures poured out, accompanied by sobbing and moaning due to my deep grief, and the tingling continued to build in intensity. When I talked about loneliness, a lifetime of pain erupted and I began to let out cries and shrieks of great intensity. They were primal screams of sadness from my depths, and I knew I was being heard by others in the house, but I didn't care anymore.

After a period of release, I would calm down, and we would talk while she held my hand. The periods of confession and release and bodily tingling continued, and my heart rate increased to amazing speed as agonies of a lifetime screamed out of me. Then came a time when I was lying on my back, exhausted, eyes closed, and doing what I do when I meditate. It seemed at one point that my heart stopped as I was drifting into the empty space of deep meditation. And then it happened.

A sudden burst of force greater than any I had ever known came pounding into my skull, throwing my chin and face skyward and backward as the power of the universe came down through the nerves at the back of my skull, and from there the force passed down through my nervous system to my heart where I could feel it regulating the rapid beat. I was totally electrified. While fully conscious, I felt every feeling, was aware of all that was happening to me, and knew I had entered a completely altered state.

I was in awe and frightened. My skull ached and my body got rigid, as if I were being electrocuted. As my heart beat at a terrifying pace, I felt roasting hot, began to sweat profusely, and my mouth became extremely dry.

In that state of paralysis my legs began rising from the table, and my arms were stiff and rising too. I was almost levitating, but part of my back and head were still touching the table. Eleanor held my left hand and forearm against her breast.

In this state I had no spasms and twitches. There was such radiant energy filling me that it is beyond my ability to describe it. I was no longer in control of my body, yet I wasn't in a trance state that separated me from the earth. I could hear voices in the next room. I was aware of Eleanor. I was conscious of my own bodily sensations.

Perhaps I was in a state of zero balance, with all forces converging on my energy system in a perfectly regulated way. But that's just speculation. I was in the realm of mystery where there are no simple, analytical explanations. All I can report is that the transition from the state of exhaustion to the feeling of being struck by lightning was sudden, as if some master switch in the universe had been thrown, and I was the circuit being electrified.

Then came four awe-inspiring words. A force beyond my own consciousness made my chest heave, and with my vocal cords and throat as a channel, created the words God has used to introduce himself to others throughout history: **"I Am Who Am."** There was a dramatic pause between each word.

It was about 5:00 p.m. and Eleanor had spent two hours preparing me. The communication from God, channeled through me, was destined to last for an hour and would end precisely at 6:00 p.m., an hour beyond the time she had set aside for my session.

Throughout that time, my radiant electrification continued and I was kept in a delicate balance at the point where eternity merges with what we call life. My experience made it clear that there is no such thing as death. There are just transitions. Death, and the fear of it, are illusions. We are eternal.

Now I will report the messages from God that I received on September 5, 1985, between 5:00 and 6:00 p.m. in Eleanor Moore's yellow farmhouse at Peterborough in the Monadnock Mountains.

I will keep it brief, and I'll include a few of my own comments here and there. Also, I will pass on to you some remarks Eleanor made in a taped interview during January 1986 when she helped me to clarify the astounding events of that special September day.

As I pass on to you the words I heard from God at Monadnock, I am using masculine pronouns for convenience. God did not specify a divine gender at Monadnock. The words of God, written as accurately as I am able to report them, are in bold type:

"I Am Who Am."

The words came from me with a pause between each word as God took over my voice apparatus and produced a single word with each heave of my chest.

I knew from my Bible reading that God introduced Himself in the same way in Chapter 3 of Exodus. "God said to Moses: I AM WHO AM."

With my heart pounding rapidly against my rib cage, chains of words paraded across my mind the way they might on a ticker tape, with God carefully selecting each word he used. He also regulated his voice to reflect his feelings. I let go of my thought-making function and put myself "on hold," and in my divinely induced paralysis, I could do nothing on my own except think some thoughts about what was going on. Every other act was God's.

Often during the session God told me, "Do not fear" and "Do not fear. You will not die." According to Eleanor, the last thing initiates into higher consciousness must overcome is death. "You can't overcome death until you overcome the fear of it."

"I Am Who Am, I am God, the One God, the God of all, the God of Love, above all gods. There are other gods. They are lesser gods, but I am over and above them. And there is One above all, over all."

This helps explain Jesus's statement that men are gods. Apparently there are many gods, with varying amounts of power. But there is one Supreme God. Eleanor speculated that the God I was in touch with was our God, but the "One above all" might be the "overall God of the planetary system." My own belief, after much reflection, is that Jesus is the Lord of this planet, that I was in touch with the God of Love who may be the Universal God referred to by Jesus as "Father," and that the "One above all" is the

Source of all that is and ever was. Theologians call this the Godhead. But how can anyone have certain knowledge of such things? All I know is what I've heard, what I've experienced. The unseen is mystery.

The next thing the voice of God said was:

"I have sent my beloved son, Jesus, to show my Love, and my beloved Jesus showed his love on the cross."

This provides the key reason for Jesus's presence on earth. Eleanor added, "Mary knew he had the Christ Spirit. When he got strong enough and aware enough, he had the same experience of tapping into the cosmic...or it tapped into him....The outside force chose him and he chose the experience. There was a connection, so he became a world figure. There are different energies, and you come out of that energy."

In a book *The Jesus Mystery* by Janet Bock, she tells of an Indian Swami who reported that God incarnated Jesus to serve as a "messenger." The swami said that in India such incarnations came when the world was in a state of distress. He said Jesus came with the message that the kingdom of heaven existed here on earth in one's own heart.

As noted, I have had visions of Jesus. And *The Jesus Mystery* was the only book I took to Rome, Jerusalem, and Cairo a year before my meeting with God at Peterborough. In that book, I underlined this passage about doubting Thomas: "Even though Thomas had been present at the raising of Lazarus and other of Jesus's miracles, he again needed to see for himself. And Jesus satisfied his need."

In Israel, Jesus resolved my own doubts as I entered Lazarus's tomb, visited The Garden, and meditated at Golgotha. Today I believe that Jesus was not exaggerating when he said, "I am the Way" and "I and my Father are one." I believe he is the Beloved Son of God, the Divine Savior of this planet, and I have tried to adopt his Way as my way.

"You, Thomas, are Horus and you are Ikhnaton. They, too, are gods. And you are the orphan son of God and will stand beside Jesus at my side in Heaven. I, too, feel like an orphan at times."

Can you imagine the awe I felt on hearing these words? Horus was a much loved god of ancient Egypt, the falcon god. In mythology texts he is "the son who is one with his father." He goes on a daily flight as the sun bird, from east to west, and every day he is reborn. Horus became an orphan when his uncle Set murdered his father Osiris and left his mother Isis a widow. Later Horus lost his eye when he tried to avenge his father's death. But he won, used his own eye to restore his father's sight, and had his own eye restored by the god Thoth's spit. The eye of Horus, to the present time, symbolizes healing.

Set later tried to discredit Horus by saying he was a bastard son, but the supreme court of the gods pronounced Horus to be the true-begotten son of his father. Before God's revelation to me about Horus, I had experienced Horus omens when reading Jung, and while in Egypt. It's amazing how God works.

"When you had your God experience on my table," Eleanor said, "and God said 'You are Horus,' he was telling you that as the orphan you are an inheritor of the Kingdom....I thought you were shown this because as a child you probably felt bad that you were an orphan....Horus was an orphan too, but he was a ruler and a principal. He was talking to your inner person. Your light, and your power, is created by God, and that's an orphan that doesn't have a physical mommy and daddy. The Horus in you is like a spark or a star or a light. God gave you the spirit of Horus and Ikhnaton."

Ikhnaton, also called Amenhotep IV, was king of Egypt around 1375 to 1358 B.C. He was a religious reformer, and was considered a heretic who believed in One God who ruled over all the earth as a kindly Father of all men. As a prophet would do, Ikhnaton spread his own belief in a loving God nearly 1400 years before Jesus arrived on the scene. The spirit of Ikhnaton in me must account for my own belief in a loving God who transcends religious boundaries.

God's statement about my role as the orphan son of God is good news for orphans, displaced persons, kids from split families, and all dispossessed people. Nobody has to feel "less than" anyone else. We all have our part to play in the drama of life.

God's comment that I will stand beside Jesus at God's side in Heaven leaves me in awe, heals any abandonment I have felt, and gives me confidence that any sacrifice on my part as I follow God's will for me is trivial compared to what's in store for me when I go home to God's loving Presence.

Also, when I recall God saying he feels like an orphan at times, this shows we have a personal God with feelings that in some way resemble the feelings

of the children he made in his image and likeness.
What a wonderful statement for God to make!

**"Gloria is a god, too, Thomas. She is Isis, and
in a mysterious way she is also Osiris. She will be
with you. Do you remember how she told you to
look at the valley of the trees and at the one star
in the sky? Do you remember the license plate you
saw after you left her? ASTRAL? She was sent to
you, Thomas. Do not fear."**

Gloria, my spirit mother, told me her birthday is
on the birth date of the Egyptian god Isis who
personifies feminine creative and healing power.
Gloria, in this incarnation, is in a healing profession.
Also, some say Christianity modeled the Mother
Mary and infant Jesus after Isis and Horus.

God's words confirmed Gloria's importance in
my life. She directed me to Monadnock, and she
remains a friend. When I reviewed this material with
Eleanor and mentioned the star Gloria had pointed
out, she said, "I wouldn't tell that to everybody."

She was trying to protect me from ridicule, but I
can't be hurt by my own truth. Those who can relate
to my truth will understand, and those who can't
relate to my story and the messages I am offering
are beyond my influence.

**"I have given everything in your life to you to
prepare you to be my prophet....In your time you
will see astounding things, things the world has
never seen....when he (Jesus) begins his 1,000-year
reign, as it is written....Everything man needs to
know is in my Word."**

The words are clear, and there is little I can add. I am reluctant to call myself a prophet, yet I accept God's will. Interpreting the word "prophet," Eleanor equated it with "messenger," and tied it to my future writing. So, to carry out God's will, I try to give messages about God's love in my writings, lectures, TV and radio work, statements during meetings of mutual help groups, and comments to individuals.

As for the "astounding things" I will see, I have already seen some "impossible" events involving the moon and the sun. But after what I experienced at Monadnock, nothing is impossible anymore.

When will the 1,000-year reign of Jesus start? I don't know. All I know is God confirmed that Jesus will come again, as the Scriptures have predicted. That's enough for me to know. The rest is mystery.

God's reference to his Word as the place to get our needs met is clear. And his Word includes the Bible, oral tradition, visions, dreams, and symbols. His Word arrives mystically in many ways, including random reading and inspired thoughts.

God can communicate in any way he pleases. He can whisper to us during meditation and prayer. And he can speak to us directly. However, he told me it was a challenge to use words. Apparently, words are very limiting. But the God of Love has no limits!

"Look on nothing with disdain. Love is in all creation."

This is a new commandment based on an old theme. It was at the core of Jesus's message to love our enemies. God paused before saying "disdain," so this word is important. It means "to despise, scorn, have aversion to, feel contempt for, to reject as unworthy of oneself...." So we must love all creation, and avoid contempt for people, places, or things. We don't have to love wrong behavior. We simply need to love each being as the creation of a loving God, and meet each person as a fellow pilgrim on the journey that will eventually bring us all home.

Obviously, whenever the God of Love creates something, God's essence is reflected in it. But it's easy for us to overlook the obvious. It's apparent that Jesus understood the Love of God as a part of all creation. Francis of Assisi understood too. They both loved all creatures, all things, all people. We, too, should love all creation as Jesus and Francis did.

"I cry to think of how they defile my gift of generation. They do not know. You will tell them, Thomas."

The key word is "gift." Since sexual generation is a sacred gift from God, we must strive for pure hearts and express love unselfishly, with tenderness and compassion, and not with greed or perversion. We must express love naturally, not unnaturally. The sexual act is for sharing affection and creating new beings, and requires kindness, consideration, and concern for each other's spiritual growth.

Sex based on real love does not include lust, demand gratification, or chase its own pleasure in a self-centered way. Love does not buy, sell, trade, or barter sexual services. Love does not degrade another to satisfy urges. Love does not utilize fear, threaten, dominate, manipulate, misuse, or abuse. Love does not achieve its aims through physical, psychological, or spiritual violence. And perhaps most important of all, sex based on love is not addictive.

We need to elevate the act of sex on this planet to the level of divine gift, sacred ritual, sacrament. The sexual connection is a God-connection worthy of divine respect and sensitivity. With the power of generation, God gave us the keys to the creation of mankind. We should protect those keys carefully.

I believe we need to clean up our sexual act and live as Jesus advised 2,000 years ago. "Love one another." If we love God, self, and others properly, our pure and unselfish hearts will radiate God's love and reflect it in all our sexual activities.

"I love everything. I love everyone. I love all, even those who do not believe. And there is no hell. I love them. Tell them how much I love them. I especially love the maimed, the deformed, the crippled, the handicapped, the addicted. I created them to give others the opportunity to love the afflicted, who will be with me in Heaven."

This tells me God's love is total. Our God of Love is not a punishing God. Instead, we punish ourselves when we separate ourselves from him with our selfishness. There may be a place somewhere in the universe with an eternal fire in it, as Jesus noted, and maybe spirits can be extinguished there in the way we burn rubbish, but a place where a spirit suffers on and on without end would not, in my view, be consistent with God's boundless love for us.

As for God's comments about afflicted people, what a wonderful explanation of why things are the way they are. God's love is at work in all situations.

Whatever happens through the use of our wills, or through accidents or diseases, God's love can make it all come out right. Also, he has a special place in his Divine Plan for those we consider unfortunate. So we need not question God's Wisdom.

"You will be with me when your work is done, Thomas. Do not worry about your heart. It will not break. You will not die. My heart is in your heart. My Love is in you."

I felt God's hand on my heart as my heart raced. My heart was pounding so hard and fast I could not imagine it surviving such an ordeal. One effect of the immense pumping of blood during the experience was that for several days following the event my ordinarily quite minor hemorrhoids bled profusely to the point where I considered buying some women's sanitary napkins. But finally the flow subsided.

During my time with God, he eased my concerns with his comments. When the thought of death entered my mind, God instantly responded to me with the helpful words he spoke through my voice apparatus. And in some instances during the session, he used thought-to-thought communication.

Throughout the entire initiation process, God encouraged me and calmed me in the depths of my paralyzed being. And when he said his heart was in my heart, I knew those words were literal. I felt a sense of unity with God that is beyond description.

God's comment that I will be with him when my work is done gives me courage to face challenges as I try to fulfill God's will for me. After all, I exist only to do God's will. It took decades trying to pursue my own will in this world to nudge me toward accepting the truth of the catechism lessons I received in childhood at St. Catherine's Sunday school. The message was hammered home that our purpose on earth was to know, love, and serve God in this world so that we would be happy with him forever in the next. The message was clear and true. I affirm it.

"You found it hard to believe what happened to Francis, but everything they say is true is true."

The "Francis" was Francis of Assisi. God did not call him a saint, as we do. He calls each of us by our first names. He certainly doesn't call us by our titles like Doctor and Professor and Reverend and General. Nor does he call us by our nicknames. I'm not "Tom," I'm "Thomas." God keeps it simple, and I believe we are all equal in his loving perspective.

When God referred to my doubts about Francis, he was showing me his knowledge of the smallest details of my life. I had doubted some of the stories about Francis, although I am a Secular Franciscan. And I also had reservations about the stigmata, or wounds of Christ, that Francis was supposed to have received from an angel. But God erased my doubts.

While my session progressed, I remained quite powerless over my body, and stayed that way for the whole hour. To show me what happened to Francis, God took my paralyzed arms and folded them in an "X" position on my chest, in the same position that is depicted on Franciscan emblems and medals.

Knowing I was radiating with God's energy and power, I identified with Francis, and realized God's truth and Francis's truth were one. Then, in slow motion, my arms began to spread, and I moved from mirroring Francis to the experience of being Jesus. I went into the crucifixion pose, with my palms facing the sky as my arms stretched out as far as they could.

Then astounding beams of energy pounded down from the heavens and I could feel them burning into my palms with laser force as I received the energy of the stigmata. I wondered if this might deform me for the rest of my life, and accepted the possibility of living with open wounds, as Francis had done.

I was sweating profusely during all this time, and the heat throughout my body was hotter than any fever I have ever felt, including the one in Israel and Egypt a year before. I also felt that the sweat coming from my forehead was actually blood. My mouth was so parched I could identify with Jesus's thirst on the cross, and I was in awe as all this happened. My awe was combined with unbelievably acute awareness.

Then, as I thought about the parched feeling on my lips and in my mouth and throat, the words of God came through me and said,

"Eleanor will moisten your lips."

Tears come as I write this passage, remembering God's tenderness. God is obviously deeply concerned with our feelings. His training may be painful, but he is not cruel. Following God's direction, Eleanor left my side and came back in a while with water. She poured some into my mouth, and it ran down my lips and onto my chin. As the "living water" touched my overheated body with its sweet coolness, it soothed me with its own life, and my being filled with joy.

I realized that even in a crucifixion there can be joy and peace, and Jesus must have had those moments despite his unspeakable agony. The Divine Presence would have made the difference for him, as it did in my symbolic crucifixion when I was electrified, paralyzed, and physically challenged. My natural body, my nervous system, and my mortal mind were enduring a trial. And God's next words reminded me of someone else's trial.

"Abraham was willing to give me his son, but I loved Abraham and he did not have to give me his son. He could keep his son and love him."

God's voice was very soft when he spoke these words. I'm not sure why he chose to tell me about Abraham. Perhaps it is to help others make sense out of the perplexing Abraham and Isaac story.

I too had to be willing to sacrifice my connection with my son when I entered a painful divorce. It was a sacrifice to be separated from him when he was only ten, and from my three daughters who were young adults. Yet, despite our separation, God enabled me and my children to nurture our love over the years, and to get to know each other as friends.

As I see it now, I think God expects us to learn to love our families and others with sincerity but also with some detachment so we don't need to control or possess them. When we truly love we should give our loved ones the freedom to move and space to grow, as our loving God gives us freedom and space.

At any rate, while still fully electrified, with my arms outstretched in the crucifixion posture, I heard the voice of God speak these words through me:

"Thomas doubted, but Thomas was loved by Jesus and was allowed to have proof of his wound. Thomas later went to India and spread the Gospel and died there....You will go to Nepal near Tibet to a monastery where you will see what I have written."

I will need direction about which monastery in Nepal to visit, and I await that guidance. As for Thomas the apostle, despite his doubt he received a special gift after the resurrection of Jesus...living proof of the reality of Jesus's wounds. And Thomas's mission to India is reflected in the existence of "Thomas Christians" there to this day.

Eleanor shared this idea with me: "Put all the apostles together and they make a whole. They make Jesus. Jesus had it all."

As God spoke to me about Thomas, the doubting apostle, my right arm rose and curled so the fingers of my right hand pressed hard against the lower part of my right rib cage. The heat at my fingertips was so intense I thought the lance wound of Jesus would be there to disfigure me for the balance of my life.

Then I heard these words:

"Only a chosen few will see the mark I have left on your chest, Thomas."

One day after this experience, in the *Illustrated Encyclopedia of Traditional Symbols* I found a picture of Jesus with the fingers of his right hand touching the wound in his right rib cage, just as my fingers had done. As I discussed this with Eleanor, she wondered if Christ's wound was "in the same place where Eve came out of Adam's rib." She thought that after my hands had been "opened up," my right hand was used to release "female creative God-Principle." She observed, "You're very male and need to release your female creative intuitive."

The mark on my chest is invisible so far, but I still remember the heat as my fingertips touched that part of my chest. And I accept what God said about a chosen few seeing the wound. Much of what God told me is mystery. But I've always loved mysteries. They make the world go around, don't they?

"Eleanor will have a mark on her chest, too. Nobody will see it. When she comes to me I will kiss it. Tell her I love her very much...."

The mark God made on Eleanor was another example of God's own knack for creating mystery. I accept God's aura of mystery, and I am simply repeating what I was told. Also, I can report that after Eleanor heard the words spoken during that special hour she told me she was pleased that she was able to hear the loving message that God had transmitted about her through my voice.

"Look at Eleanor, Thomas. Open your eyes."

The light dazzled my eyes, and its radiance was simply incredible. How can I describe that light? That astounding light from the heavens? It was the light of all lights, from the source of all light. It was the wonder of all wonders. The very thought of it fills me with awe, and the memory of it makes my eyes feel like squinting. At any rate, right after I had opened my eyes, I was told,

"Do not be afraid, Thomas. You will not go blind."

The light of God's Presence was so astoundingly bright I will never forget it. Gold? Silver? White? I don't know. Probably a mixture of gold and white. I'm not sure. I just know it was amazingly bright.

My head began to turn, through God's direction, in a jerky fashion. I was not moving it. Whatever the self is, it was suspended now, and had no place in the initiation ceremony. Eternal energy was doing the moving. And I was fully conscious of that energy and how it was in charge of my slightest movements. As I looked at where Eleanor was sitting, God's voice said,

"You will not see her."

Where Eleanor had been sitting, there was no Eleanor. I was seeing right through her bodily form, and for a while she remained invisible. I could see only the wall and bookcases behind her.

Then, bit by bit, she appeared in miniature, low in my field of vision, and finally she expanded into normal size like a balloon being inflated. When I discussed this incident with her months later, she said, "I've done that to other people. I've disappeared in front of a room full of people a couple of times."

I asked, "Is that God's way of telling us that everything's an illusion?"

"Yes, everything is not what you think it is."

This event led me to remember that I have had other experiences where friends seemed to disappear before my eyes in large rooms of people. But I never truly believed they had disappeared. I chalked it up to a blind spot in my field of vision. Maybe I saw through their bodily forms.

Another fascinating experience took place in St. Mary's Church, Dedham. I was at Mass with my son, and during the "Peace to you" greeting, I turned and behind me I saw a man's face that was a mass of scarred flesh with tiny holes where a nose should have been, and a smaller than usual mouth opening. The only things that seemed intact were his eyes. I looked into those eyes, said "Peace," reached out my hand to shake his, and felt only a stump.

I smiled nervously, went back to attending to the Mass, went to Communion, and on my return to the pew the man was gone. I'm not saying he dissolved into thin air. My son saw him too, so I know it was not a hallucination. But one minute he was there, and the next he was gone. It reminded me a bit of Francis of Assisi meeting a leper and touching him.

As for the "impossible" things that happened to me at Peterborough, I say this: "My belief system has lost its boundaries. I now believe in the impossible."

The former me would have had a difficult time saying those words. It has taken a series of mystical experiences to change me so I can accept events that defy the laws of logic. I once worked hard at being logical, and often my logical part thought it controlled my destiny. Now I see that my so-called logical thinking was just a sincere delusion.

I believe today that God's logic differs from ours. And although it may sound a bit like determinism, I believe God chooses the parts we are to play in this planetary drama. What about our free will? Well, I guess we are free to play our part or run from it. The catch is that when we run from our own destiny it leaves us feeling more uncomfortable than when we simply accept God's will for us.

In any case, after Eleanor had gradually returned to full size, the room was still filled with dazzling light, and I felt so hot that when I touched something metal on her wrist, I thought it would certainly melt.

Looking back, it seems that in my altered state I was conscious of two realities at once. I knew I was still in space and time, yet I knew I was functioning beyond space and time, in eternity.

Eleanor's presence in the room was real to me, and so was God's presence. Also, the awe-inspiring flow of electrical energy through me could not be ignored. It was so powerful that it definitely caught my attention. And the beat of my heart throughout the whole session was so strong that it felt like it would pound right through the wall of my chest. It was pounding the way a heart pounds after a long workout on a treadmill in a cardiologist's laboratory.

As for time, there was no way for me to measure time during my special hour with God. It was only after the hour was over that I could begin to get any perspective on it. That particular hour had a timeless aspect to it.

Speaking of time, I have to admit that I often get confused by God's time. And I wonder when God will fulfill the various revelations he made to me at Monadnock. But I know in my heart that God's time is the best time. So all I have to do is fulfill my own duty to God by carrying the messages he gave me on September 5, 1985.

In addition, I want to make it clear to readers that just because I had a special experience of God, that doesn't mean I have become superhuman. Instead, I think it has made me even more sensitive to the challenges of life. I still have to cope with my allergies and other health problems. And I have my bouts with anxiety.

However, I'm not as much a victim of feelings as before. I am more in tune with God's will today. So I am much more peaceful. I believe some of that peace comes directly from God, some of it comes from Jesus, and some comes from Mary.

"Mary is a god. She had one child, Jesus. They think she had more. They do not know."

The message speaks for itself. If God says Mary is a god, then that's all there is to it. Apparently, the theological speculation about Jesus having brothers is wasted energy. Why do people want to believe that Mary had more children? Can't they handle the idea of a virgin birth? With God all things are possible.

Several times during the session, God said to me,

"Smile, Thomas, I am a God who smiles."

At one point, God took my mouth and my lips and forced a large smile onto my face! What can I say? Isn't it wonderful to think of a God who smiles? God loves. God smiles. God enjoys informality and the light touch. He even uses the word "okay."

When I wondered about what I would be called on to do as his prophet, God just said,

"Do not worry. Easy does it. They will come to you."

Apparently I am supposed to take it one day at a time, letting my life unfold, and being open to the people who come into it. This means that much of the time I must keep my natural curiosity restrained, and hold back my inclination to get right into tasks and get things done. Often I ask God, "When?" The reply tends to be silence. The indirect message is, "Just do your best, and wait."

"Gloria will be with you. Other women will come and follow you as they followed Jesus."

I continue my connection with Gloria as the years go by, and a number of other special women have come into my life. In truth, I believe women have an important place in God's spiritual planning. When it comes to spirituality, women tend to be more enthusiastic and receptive than men. I have shared information such as the contents of this book with women, and they have been grateful. Also, some women, during lectures I've given, have seen my aura, been amazed by it, and told me about it.

"You will teach them to meditate as I have taught you to meditate."

The meditation I practice is not complicated, and is silent, sitting meditation based on the discipline encouraged by a Benedictine monk, John Main. He learned to do it in India and eventually brought it to the Benedictine monastery in Montreal. Then, until his death, he did his best to spread the word about it.

You sit with legs crossed on a little pillow on the floor, or in a chair with arms. You let your hands rest in your lap, with fingers touching lightly. And you may choose to use some beads, such as rosaries or the meditation beads of the Far East. If you doze off, they will drop, slide against the edge of your chair or hit the floor, and will wake you up.

You close your eyes lightly, let your eyes aim down the bridge of your nose, notice your breathing, and as you breathe in and out through your nose, with mouth closed, you say or hear your prayer word, or mantra, without actually moving your lips. You actually think your mantra...until it fades away.

As you sit with eyes closed, seeming to look out of a dark cave through your forehead, you don't look for pictures on the screen of your vision. Instead, you work quietly to clean off that visual screen so it's blank. When your thoughts disappear, your mind is left clear and connected with God, in the silence.

The mantra, or prayer word, is our spiritual tool. We simply listen to it, or think it. The best mantras don't conjure up a visual image. I use "Maranatha" and "AUM," pronounced "Ahh...ooh...mmmmm." The mantra clears the mind, brings peace, and helps to bring mystical union with God.

I breathe deeply into my abdomen, let it expand slowly, and watch my breathing. I repeat my mantra until it fades and leaves me in the deep silence with God. I do this twice a day, from 20 to 30 minutes, in the early morning and late in the day. I do this on an empty stomach and without caffeine, but I take some orange juice to help me stay awake in the morning. And I usually use beads to help keep me alert.

The condition I aim for is alert stillness. No preliminary exercises are needed. The goal? To do, think, and say nothing. Usually there are moments when no messages enter the mind, and that is just fine. And sometimes messages come, like the one I received: "The work comes first, everything else second." The "work" is meditation itself, or yoga, which means scientific union with God.

There are many views on the value of meditation. Eleanor believed that it provided "a way of releasing energy, getting rid of garbage, and becoming more aware of the inner person." I believe we each receive spiritual benefits from the practice, and if we do it consistently, it has the power to change our lives.

In my English Composition course at Cape Cod Community College, I give a writing assignment that includes reading about meditation, trying it, and then writing about it. For most students, it is their first real attempt to sit and be still, and yet they are able to write about benefits received even after only a few minutes in deep silence based on alert stillness.

As my session with God continued, I received additional emphasis from God about my role in his grand design.

"Now, Thomas, you will be my prophet."

According to Eleanor, a prophet was "a witness or messenger." She explained, "Your old soul that burned up its shit and garbage and fear can very objectively look and see the patterns of what is going on around the planet today....You'll write your experiences. Part of your experience was knowing that you are a book. You're the Book of Life. I am too. We've been around more than once." She was referring to prior lives. Past lives were as real to Eleanor as the present life is to most people.

"Look at the ceiling, Thomas."

The light was incredibly bright, almost blinding, and in the rough plaster of the ceiling I saw a configuration that looked very much like the outline of Italy. It seemed to be in the shape of a boot, or high shoe. It truly captured my attention for a time, and then came the words:

"Do not be afraid, Thomas."

Astounding energy poured through me, and it seemed to come out from my eyes like a powerful penetrating ray. Then came these words:

"You will not go blind."

Repeatedly during the experience, I suspended my fear. When fear entered my mind, it was like a bug flying by, and my awareness of God's loving connection with me removed it.

Then God began to use my eyes in what seemed a very odd way, yet after eye surgery the previous winter I had experienced something similar. On that occasion, my anesthetized eye had seen images that were different from those seen by my active eye. And it was a bit frightening to have that happen.

As I lay there at Eleanor's watching the image on the ceiling, God took my eyes, and a concentrated beam of energy, like a laser, came from one eye and poured onto the place on the ceiling to which he had directed my vision. During this time, God's thoughts kept flooding into my mind, advising me to hold on and not let go of the intense gaze. I held on.

"There will be a mark."

The light of God apparently left a mark on that ceiling. Months later, Eleanor told me that some of the people coming to see her since my visit had been fascinated by the ceiling. "I have more aware people coming here now." As for the word "mark," she said it could mean "the Word that all words stem from."

"It is finished."

In a dramatic way, pausing between each word, God's statement echoed Jesus's words on the cross. Those words come after completion of the experience of initiation into higher consciousness.

Eleanor left the room for a while after the three words were spoken, but my inner experience went on. The power of God lifted my stiff body into a sitting position, and as I was propped up by my extended arms, some private messages came. And my eyes were then directed toward objects in the room, with one eye used to project the beam, or ray.

The radiant energy continued to fill me as my eyes went to a picture of Francis of Assisi on a table near the door. Then my eyes went to a blue, white, and gold ceramic unicorn. The ray from my eye rested on its horn, and I thought the ceramic might explode. Also, my eye sent a ray to the light switch on the wall. Months later, Eleanor told me that since my visit people had developed interest in Francis' picture and in the unicorn.

Each time my head moved during this time, it had a jerky motion. I was not moving it; it was being moved. Next, in an obscure nook to the rear of where

Eleanor had been sitting at my left, I saw an artistic oversized postcard with an angelic figure on it, and rays of heavenly light coming from it. Before I left Eleanor's place that evening, she gave me that postcard depicting Metatron, the Archangel of the Presence who came to Moses.

Sitting there, I was sweating profusely, getting small chains of words from God that seemed to be transition comments, bringing me back to everyday reality. And as my mobility returned, the altered state diminished in intensity. Yet my body was still pulsating with electrical energy. I actually thought I was sweating blood, and I was tingling all over as I tugged at my shirt, popping a button on it. I used part of it to wipe my forehead, and then expected to see blood on the shirt. There was none there.

I was feeling like a giant as I sat there alone, still filled with much tingling energy. Moving stiffly to the floor, I felt much larger than life, but with a very deep fatigue. I flung myself onto the divan, and curled up there, wanting to sleep but knowing that I had to stay awake. As I lay recovering, my mind was whirling with thoughts of what had just happened to me. In those moment my whole being was filled with God's words of love. I knew it was my destiny now to carry the awareness of my God of Love to others.

I had come a long way from being Thomas the doubter. "My God, what a God you are!" I thought as I lay there with God's words flying through my mind. As memories of the experience flooded in, I reflected, "It's beyond belief, but it's true."

When Eleanor came back into the room, she said, "That was quite a trip you took." She told me she had been blessed by my experience. And when this mystic who saw people's auras or "lights" examined me, she saw a cross in the middle of my forehead where some say the eye of the soul is located.

I died symbolically on the cross during my initiation experience that day, and I believe a new Thomas replaced the former one. I was filled with a new sense of unity and wholeness, and I knew now that my life was no longer my own. It was God's.

The cross symbolizes sacrifice. We must crucify our selfishness as we prepare for Jesus's return, when he will rule in peace and love for a thousand-year reign such as this world has never known.

At the end of my session with Eleanor, she told me to stay on the divan, resting, until I felt able to get up. Soon, as the tingling sensations lessened, I was able to sit up and retrieve the objects I had taken off. I also picked up the manila folder containing items I hadn't needed to refer to. On the way out she introduced me to her husband and daughter, but I was so dazed I could hardly walk, talk, or speak.

After exchanging a hug with Eleanor, I left the yellow farmhouse in a dreamlike state. It was about 7:00 p.m. and raining heavily as I drove back toward Massachusetts after experiencing God's crucible of heavenly fire. A few miles away I passed a large building in flames. I was transformed by fire, and so was somebody's property, at nearly the same time.

As I drove, the monotonous swish of windshield wipers was hypnotic, and I took a wrong turn that led me to Manchester, the long way home. I had managed to get lost on the way up that morning, but arrived at my destination, and here I was, getting lost again. But I had a safe trip home.

On the way I scribbled notes about my experience on a pad beside me. At times I would pull over to the side of the road and write rapidly as my mind flooded with detailed memories of the experience. Late that evening, beyond midnight, I sat with my tape recorder and spoke more details into it, while writing down notes, and then I paused. When I started to tape again I forgot to press the red record button. And I continued talking for a long time. It was not recording, but at least I was getting my notes together and reinforcing my memory.

At home I spent days compiling my notes on the experience, and did some cutting and pasting to arrange them in a readable sequence.

I had a deep heaviness pressing on my chest for a full week after Monadnock, the same kind of feeling I get when I am grieving an extreme loss. I felt weak and exhausted in the aftermath of the experience that had made me feel larger than life for a brief time.

In a book on Francis of Assisi's life, I learned that he too experienced a combination of fright and joy after his communion with God. I also read words indicating his belief in the idea of many gods. "You are the one Lord God above all the Gods," he wrote. Reviewing Francis's experience of the stigmata, I no longer doubted what had happened to him.

After Monadnock, I reviewed many books, and I saw new meaning in comments that had previously held little interest. In *The Jesus Mystery* by Janet Bock, these words struck me: "All human beings are proceeding along an evolutionary path which will eventually culminate in the goal of mergence with God....some are further along than others."

Flipping *Gray's Anatomy* open at random, I learned that the 10th pneumogastric nerve supplies the organs of voice and respiration, the pharynx, esophagus, stomach, and heart. This led me to believe that the universal energy followed that path after it entered my skull at the fontanel, then put me into the proper state, and provided the power system over which God's voice traveled. I read about the pineal gland, optic thalami, and medulla oblongata, which serve as a bridge from God to man during meditation, or in an experience like mine.

Also, in medieval philosophy I once read that the ancients viewed the pineal gland as the seat of the soul, and I have read that when autopsies are done a sandy crystalline substance is found in that gland. I wonder if this substance provides crystal power like that of a computer chip, and gives us the way to communicate with our Creator.

In *The Urantia Book*, a text recommended by a mystic I met while visiting North Conway, New Hampshire, I read about Jesus's "transfiguration" on Mount Hermon. He announced to three apostles one afternoon at three o'clock that he was leaving them "to commune with the Father and His messengers." Jesus returned at six o'clock. And my experience with Eleanor had begun at about 3:00 p.m. and had ended at 6:00 p.m. An interesting coincidence.

On Jesus's return from his meeting with God, he said, "I now declare that the Son of Man has chosen to go through his full life in your midst as one of you. Be of good cheer; I will not leave you until my work is finished." God also told me that I will return to him only when my "work" here is finished.

On the Sunday following my Monadnock trip, at St. Mary's Church in Dedham, I flipped the Mass book open at random, and before my eyes I saw the page headed "Transfiguration." It said, "In the shiny cloud the Spirit is seen. From it the voice of the Father is heard. 'This is my son, my beloved son, in whom is all my delight. Listen to him.'" God described Jesus to me as his "beloved son" too.

In *Edgar Cayce on Reincarnation*, I read about Jesus reviving the teachings of the Essenes, beliefs "rooted firmly in the laws of reincarnation." Jesus, in the Gospels, referred to the belief in reincarnation without criticizing it, so the revelation that I am a blend of former spirits known as Horus and Ikhnaton is consistent with my Christianity.

On September 19, I flipped open a copy of the Psalms and here is what I read in Psalm 82: "God presides in the heavenly council; in the meeting of the gods (interesting use of the plural) He gives his decision." Then in the Scriptures I read, "I told you that you are gods, that all of you are the sons of the Most High." Again, the plural "gods" is used.

In *Tantra in Tibet*, I read: "If a phenomenon, such as a body, and its emptiness were exactly the same, then when we saw the body, we would see its emptiness." Maybe that's what I saw when God told me to look at Eleanor, and said I would not see her.

In *Psychology and Religion* by Carl Jung, I read: "Religious experience is absolute. It is indisputable. No matter what the world thinks about religious experience, the one who has it possesses the great treasure of a thing that has provided him with a source of life, meaning and beauty and that has given a new splendor to the world and to mankind."

The book *Men Who Have Walked With God*, written by Sheldon Cheney, reported on the mystic visions of Catherine of Siena, whose name was attached to the church I attended in Norwood as a child. Catherine was described as being "rapt out of her corporeal senses" as information came to her "dictated by God the Father." She also said she was "transformed into Christ."

Later, in *Christ Consciousness*, a journal written by Norman Paulsen, I found a report that reminded me of my own experience at Monadnock: "forces beyond my poor control"...."incredible voice".... "incredible light"...."Tremendous vibrations"...."I couldn't move my body"...."beyond the barriers of time, space and images."

Paulsen wrote, "As Moses saw God face to face, so did I, and so can you." He said that meditation is the vehicle to use in preparation for the experience.

As the days following my experience of God passed, I read at random in the Scriptures often, and here are some of the messages I received: "Write therefore the things thou hast seen and the things that are, and the things that are to come hereafter." "No one can question what you have done or challenge your judgment." "Tell your fellow exiles what I am saying." "Pack your bundle for exile."

Shortly afterward, I moved to Cape Cod. My first day on the Cape was Columbus Day, October 12, 1985. Like Columbus, I knew where I was going, but didn't know what would happen when I arrived. Yet much of my life has been that way. After all, on the day I went to see Eleanor Moore in the Monadnock Mountains I also knew where I was going, but I certainly didn't expect to meet God there.

10
Beyond the Mountains

On Cape Cod it took me nearly two years to develop and refine the 220 page manuscript telling the story of my meeting with God. Recently, I have condensed it to make it less expensive to publish. At first I wanted to shout about it to the whole world, but each time I felt that way I remembered God's counsel to take it easy and wait for the appropriate people to come into my life. That gave me peace.

At the interview with Eleanor Moore in January 1986, I gained new perspective on Monadnock. One item was the connection between my experience of God and the kundalini, a yoga component visualized in Asia as a circular, spiral, coiling, winding serpent slumbering at the base of the spine, and waiting to be roused. One of the aims of yoga meditation is to rouse the serpent, get her to lift her head, and bring her up a subtle nerve along the spine to the crown of the head. When this happens, energies of contrary powers come together and bring a transformation in the individual.

We discussed this powerful transforming force, and the meditation I had been practicing for a long time prior to my visit. She said I had been "all uptight and full of tensions" when our session had begun. "Your electrical energy was shut off because you had experienced so much tension. You were electrocuted to bring you back to life."

She compared my experience to the Frankenstein story. "We're supposed to have an electrical force that's part of our lives and goes out to heal people, but for many people it's pinched off. As you began to relax you began to feel the flow. Once you began to feel it, it connected you with the earth. You felt energy in your feet and you said, 'Something's coming up through my feet,' because you had tapped into the power of the planet itself."

Eleanor said my screaming was "what happens when the kundalini comes up the spine and up through the chakras and opens your throat. You yell and yell and yell, and when it rings like a bell and I hear it go outside the room and out into the whole area, then I know that as far as anybody can hear that tone they'll come to you to learn what you went through. You'll be their teacher."

She compared the yelling to a newborn baby clearing its lungs, and said that after my screaming I became very peaceful. "Then you got whapped again. That's when the energy came up again and opened the doors in your head, and lightning came in and revitalized your heart and brought heaven and earth together. You, as a human being, went through a death and a rebirth. You died and came right back. Now you're a new person. You're not exactly who you were before. A lot of garbage in you was burned out, including your old fears and anxieties. You're not afraid of death anymore. And the resentment and negativity about being an orphan got burned up."

She said many people came to her to release kundalini. "That's similar to you going through your God experience. But they may not be as advanced as you are to go through the last phases of it. They may be just releasing energy on a baby level. You went through last initiation, overcoming death."

On the subject of the paralysis I felt during the initiation experience, and the voice that came out of me, she said, "The Energy and the Power were choosing your words and using your voice box."

The time I spent interviewing Eleanor was very beneficial. I have often reviewed the tape I made with her that day. It's all the more special now that she has gone back home to God's Heaven, and is not available to me in person.

After interviewing Eleanor, I took considerable time to sift through the experience, and continued my mystical research as I went along with life in the worlds of family, work, and personal growth.

Each time I was afflicted by the notion that the world was eagerly waiting for my good news, the message God gave me about taking it easy motivated me not to rush. So I lived a day at a time, trying to practice the counsels I had received at Monadnock, and I slowly but surely organized the materials that would eventually come together as a book telling about my time of direct communication with God.

When I had the manuscript under way, I became interested in publishing it, and when I discussed it with Gloria on Cape Cod, she advised me to write under an assumed name. So I did, out of humility. When the book was done, I gave a copy to about 30 friends who seemed quite underwhelmed by my spiritual experience. This surprised me, but provided another dose of humility, which is an important part of our spiritual journey.

Reviewing the lives of others who had met God directly, I saw their pattern of going on with life, facing rejection undaunted, and still keeping their mission in the forefront of their minds no matter how long it took to reach the goals assigned to them. So I went on with my life, and tried in a subtle way at times, and in a more dramatic way at other times, to carry God's messages in my writing and lecturing, and in private communication during the years that have passed since September 5, 1985.

During these years I have been active in writers' groups. I was president of the New England Chapter of the American Medical Writers Association, and co-authored *Biomedical Communication: Selected AMWA Workshops*. I am a member of the Twelve O'Clock Scholars group on Cape Cod, and served a while as program director of the Cape Cod Writers' Conference. Also, I was president of Professional Writers of Cape Cod. I have gained much inspiration and fellowship in these affiliations.

After settling on Cape Cod, I continued to write features each month for the *U.S. Journal of Drug and Alcohol Dependence*, where I was a national correspondent. But that kind of journalism did not give me the opportunity to spread my own opinions or reflections because I had to report objectively.

Then in January of 1986 The Cape Cod Times agreed to let me try a column titled "On Addiction." It caught on, and appeared each Thursday until the end of 1998, reaching between 50,000 and 100,000 readers, depending on just how many tourists were around. So I had an audience for my insights into addiction and spirituality. Now I write a column on Health/Lifestyle for The Cape Cod Journal, on-line.

Because I believe the addictions that afflict us are the modern version of the idol worship cautioned against in ancient times, I have chosen addiction writing as my specialty. Also, I have produced videos on the subject at C3TV on Cape Cod, a community television station where I am a member. My series "Understanding Addiction" airs often.

At Cape Cod Community College I developed a community services course in addiction, and one on healthy intimacy, which is so important in addiction recovery. This has given me the opportunity to mention spirituality very often, because addictions are essentially a spiritual problem. Actually, the most effective recoveries from addiction I am aware of are those based on having a spiritual awakening.

As time passed, the spiritual messages I heard at Monadnock became integrated into my being, and so they have found their way into every aspect of my life since that wonderful hour of divine Revelation.

When I served as communications consultant to Beech Hill Hospital, an addiction treatment center in the Monadnocks, I was able to inject some spiritual material into their newsletter because the hospital is founded on the basis of the Twelve Steps initiated by Alcoholics Anonymous. Also, in lectures to church and community groups, I have been able to carry a spiritual message. As a group instructor in a driver alcohol education program at Cape Counseling Center in Hyannis, I was able to encourage spiritual growth through Twelve Step Program participation.

In addition, an emphasis on the development of the human spirit has been at the core of the books I have published since 1990: *Addicted? A Guide to Understanding Addiction*; *Improving Intimacy: 10 Powerful Strategies*; *The Odd Duck, a Story for Odd People of All Ages*; and my metaphysical novel, *Danny The Prophet*. Also, there was a spiritual component in the booklet I wrote for Hazelden in

Minnesota, *Up in Smoke*. It has reached nearly 20,000 smokers, helped many to quit, and has brought me much satisfaction.

I have felt much joy passing on the good news drawn from my experience at Monadnock. During these years of attempting to be useful to God I have tried to conform to God's will, have often prayed for patience and endurance, and for a long time I have wanted to do a concise report on my Monadnock adventure, including information on my own life. It feels right to be writing it now, after more than 10 years have passed since my meeting with God. And my insights have matured.

The years since 1985 have been a fascinating adventure for me, one day at a time. I have utilized Twelve Step groups for my spiritual development, along with my daily practice of prayer, meditation, and spiritual reading. Also, in addition to being a Catholic and a member of the Secular Franciscan Order, I am in a Unitarian Universalist fellowship where I find a deep sense of loving community. I see no conflict in this duality. God has no boundaries.

At this juncture I want to make it clear that I have not become perfect since my experience of intimate communication with God. On the contrary, I am aware each day of how human I am, though wonderfully connected with my Source.

I have experienced life in all its variety. I have had fun, joy, and great happiness since that special hour in September of 1985. I have also been sad, disappointed, frustrated, and subject to the whole range of moods that come with being human.

Also, I have been confronted by danger. In a snowstorm at Dublin, New Hampshire, late at night, driving alone down the mountain where Beech Hill Hospital is located, time stood still for me in 1990 when my car went out of control and spun in many circles, coming to rest at the edge of a steep precipice, with no guard rail for protection.

On the weekend when my car went into a spin, I also learned that Beech Hill Hospital was curtailing my services as a consultant. And soon my income descended toward the poverty line. Descending into drastic underemployment, or "downward mobility," I went bankrupt. And this was not pleasant for one who had been proud of self-reliance and an excellent credit rating. But God saw me through it.

I experienced a different kind of danger during one Christmas season. Accepting an invitation to have tea and cookies in a beautiful home on Cape Cod, I found out what it is like to be in a house that goes up in flames. It was only a matter of minutes between the time the Christmas tree caught fire to the point where all available oxygen was gone, and my lungs stopped functioning. Although this was a life-threatening situation, I came through unscathed, except for some post-traumatic stress reactions later.

During the past couple of years I have had to confront a serious threat to my health. Cancer of the prostate. After exploring various options I decided on radical surgery, which I believed to be the wisest course. At the same time, the ordeal of preparing for and recovering from a five-hour surgical procedure gave me one of the major endurance tests of my life.

Shortly after returning home to Cape Cod after hospitalization at Lahey Hitchcock Clinic, I woke up one morning with my left leg very swollen. I had a life-threatening blood clot in a problematic location high up my leg. This led to hospitalization at Cape Cod Hospital, followed by several months of blood samples, medication, and a continuing feeling of vulnerability. But God provided the strength and nourishment in the form of loving friends and relatives, and additional spiritual growth...and trust.

These and other experiences, I believe, had to be part of my ongoing education in this adventure we call life. Having a dramatic spiritual experience does not mean that everything in life becomes easy. But it does help one achieve acceptance of God's will.

Also, the *U.S. Journal of Drug and Alcohol Dependence*, which I served for eight years, became a casualty of the recession a few years ago, and went out of business. It was another large loss to grieve. I felt that I was really in my element doing that kind of journalistic work, and it was a labor of love.

Regardless of losses, I believe that each moment, whether pleasant or unpleasant, has its meaning in God's Divine Plan for my life, and all events are significant in one way or another. Each happening is both a gift and a lesson, and is either God's direct will for me or his permissive will.

Today, when things happen in strange or painful ways, I try to remember what the two anonymous women in England said in the book *God Calling*: "Appreciation results from contrary experience."

I have seen the link between negative events and positive outcomes. For example, bankruptcy and underemployment led me to perform more part-time teaching at Cape Cod Community College, where I have been on the adjunct faculty as a writing instructor since 1988. And working at the College has become a very satisfying way of life.

When all efforts to attract new clients during the recession of 1990 and 1991 didn't pan out, I taught more courses at the College, and was later led into a part-time position as writing coach and mentor for business students, a fulfilling role. I've been able to share my insights, abilities, and love with those who have difficulty expressing themselves in writing. This would not have happened without my financial decline and fall several years ago.

Also, downward mobility and financial distress have enhanced my appreciation of simple things such as a tasty peanut butter sandwich. Now in my mid-sixties, I'm in the early years of retirement within the Social Security system that I have been paying into since age 14, and I am learning about the challenges of survival when faced with income limitations set by government and bordering on the bizarre. It can be a very strange adventure at times.

Today the only "assets" and possessions I have are spiritual ones. I have very little money on reserve in a bank. I live from day to day precariously, as billions of others do. In a partnership with God, I just do my best and let God do the rest. God takes care of my needs. I've learned to live with much and with little. And I need not fear either condition.

The main thing I have learned is not to become too attached to wealth when I have it, and to share it and keep it flowing. It has been good for me to relieve myself of attachment to tangibles. And now that I have detached, I don't believe it would pose a spiritual problem to move to less precarious living at some future time. Meanwhile, I am grateful for the gifts I receive every day, and I thank God for them--

* God's Love, Truth, and Compassion.

* My spiritual journey and my sobriety.
* My family, friends, and colleagues.
* My health, healing, mobility, and creativity.
* My senses, my sensitivity, and my serenity.
* My food, clothing, and shelter.
* My transportation and useful work.
* And all the other gifts God has given me.

At this moment, I thank God for the time and the ability to write this account of my spiritual journey. And I thank God for each reader, while hoping that it helps you in your own spiritual journey. In the end, all you have to do is be yourself, your real self, the self connected to your Creator, the God of Love.

11
Memories and Reflections

As I bring this journal to its conclusion, I have a few memories and reflections to share with you. Since September 5, 1985, I have had much time to reflect on my life before the Monadnock Revelations, the power of that special time with Eleanor Moore, and later experiences.

I recall how skeptical I once was about people's dramatic spiritual conversions. Well, that skepticism has gone. And I no longer have doubts about the story of Jesus, and the stigmata of Francis of Assisi.

Once I thought God had lost touch with this planet and was active elsewhere. Now I believe God is personal, always present, and his radiance never stops. He is like the blazing sun, we are like rays of light coming directly from him, and the connection is constant. God and his Love are always there, though our awareness changes.

Once I thought in terms of our limitations as humans. Now, after experiencing the impossible at Monadnock, I think we are eternal light beings in temporary bodies. We're sons and daughters of an unconditionally loving God.

There was a time when I connected punishment with God. Now I see that we are the ones who punish others and punish ourselves for wrongdoing. And when we act in unloving ways, we feel separated from God and create our own hell. But God loves us, with all of our flaws, and never abandons us.

As for the future, I was told I'll see things the world has never seen. Also, I was told that Jesus is going to return, just as it was written in the Scriptures. So we don't have to worry. All we have to do is live fully in the present, in God's Presence.

To live fully in the present, we need to practice the Presence of God without ceasing, with prayer as our way of life. We need to turn our lives into an ongoing prayer by meditating silently from 20 to 30 minutes each morning, and again later in the day. If each person in the world did this, we all would be channels for God's peace and love.

Also, since prayer and meditation are antidotes for addiction, and because we are all addicted to a degree, world health would be vastly improved by widespread adoption of these practices demonstrated by Jesus, his followers, and other spiritual leaders.

Prayer and meditation help us realize that God is always with us, and waits patiently for us to find his Presence. But we cannot realize his Presence while we are chasing addictive illusions that interfere with our spiritual growth. Addictions distract us from our purpose in life, which is to know, love, and serve

God. We're not here to attach ourselves addictively to money, power, perfection, alcohol, drugs, food, sex, gambling, work, or other behaviors.

Through meditation, the path of love, we gain a quiet understanding of ourselves, while developing compassion for others, and we develop sincere and deep love of God. We learn to crucify our selfishness and replace it with love, and that brings us an inner sense of oneness, a sense of unity with others, and a sense of God being one with us. Meditate and pray as if your life depends on it. It does!

As for prophecies about the end of the world being near, this is all in the realm of mystery. Who understands it? God does, nobody else. But I heard God say Jesus is returning, and that, to me, is good news. I also believe we have been in the end times for a while now. We have all the signs around us. But while we see great disasters, we also see wonders of spiritual renewal. So I look forward to the end of this world, but not as obliteration of the planet. I see it as the loving fulfillment of the Divine Plan.

Jesus will guide us into the most wonderful time since the Garden of Eden. There we were innocent, lost our innocence, and were alienated from God. Soon we'll return to planetary innocence and take our place in God's universe of light. Meanwhile, we need only live, pray, meditate, and love.

On January 18, 1986, when I was interviewing Eleanor Moore about my initiation experience, she told me I was going to become more aware of God's Kingdom, the invisible world, here on Earth. That has happened. She said I would "realize there's a beautiful sparkling world right here in this heavy physical one." She was right.

Discussing meditation, she said sometimes in deep meditation a light like a star appears, very tiny and very bright. I see this gold white light sometimes as I meditate, and I feel its wondrous glow.

On Christ consciousness, she explained, "It's the part of me that's gold and loves you with no strings attached and loves the whole universe. It's God's love! It's gold light and white light. It's so powerful! First you're aware of it in yourself as it goes out to other people. Then you're aware that it's going all over the planet. It taps into the universal and I believe Jesus did that and came to show that to you as a person."

When we discussed Jesus's role in ushering this planet into a new era when he begins his 1,000-year reign, she said, "I think every 2,000 years the planet goes out of its space and into new space and has to go through a death and a rebirth." She mentioned Moses taking people through a major transition, and Jesus taking the world through a similar one. Horus, the Falcon God, according to ancient legend, is supposed to return one day to be part of such a transition. Since God said I am Horus, then I'm here as part of the transition team.

The crucifixion I experienced at Monadnock, according to Eleanor, was "letting go of the ego, burning it away." What is left then, she explained, is "love." The love gained during the process makes the pain of ego deflation easier to deal with.

Discussing the power that came pounding out of the heavens and cast its beams into the palms of my hands and other parts of my body, she said they were "rods of power" with healing energy in them.

As for the cross on my forehead, she said the cross symbolizes clairvoyance. "The center of your head opens and you put the God light out to bless people. It comes out to do healing and to see with."

She saw my life on Earth this way: "The prodigal son leaves home and has a lot of experiences and then goes back home." I recall how gently Eleanor explained that God gives us our energy and says to us, "Here's the energy. Do what you want with it and when you're done with it you give it back."

God hopes we have wide experience with the energy, and forgives us in advance for the mistakes we make with it. So the important thing, I believe, is to live fully, not fearfully, one day at a time.

As a journalist, my writing assignment is pretty much done now, and my mission as a prophet or messenger of God will continue until the rest of my work is done and I go home to his loving Presence. I see each day of my work for God as an adventure. And I feel the same way about people and events.

Meanwhile, if you wonder how far we are supposed to go when we climb the mountain to meet God, please reflect on a comment by an eminent scientist in the field of biology.

Dr. Lewis Thomas, from the Memorial Sloan-Kettering Cancer Center in New York, wrote these important words about recombinant DNA in the New England Journal of Medicine: "Is there something fundamentally unnatural, or intrinsically wrong, or hazardous for the species, in the ambition that drives us all to reach a comprehensive understanding of nature, including ourselves? I cannot believe it.

"It would seem a more unnatural thing, and more of an offense against nature, for us to come on the same scene endowed as we are with curiosity, filled to overbrimming with questions, and naturally talented as we are for the asking of clear questions, and then for us to do nothing about it, or worse, to try to suppress the questions.

"This is the greatest danger to our species, to try to pretend that we are another kind of animal, that we do not need to satisfy our curiosity, exploration and experimentation, and that the human mind can rise above its ignorance by simply asserting that there are things it has no need to know."

I think we can apply this powerful thinking to the world of the spiritual quest and its mysteries. All my life, to a greater or lesser degree, I have wondered about God, studied texts about God, and explored psychology and philosophy and mysticism, in a quest for spiritual growth and understanding. So I believe there is no substitute for individual research.

When we discover the God in each of us, we change from uncomfortable solitary beings to people with a wonderful sense of unity. When we find God in us, and know he is also out there beyond us, we break through barriers of time and space, entering a new dimension of being in which the impossible becomes possible, the incredible becomes believable, and we are left in awe of the God of Love who created this planet and rules over it in a kindly way.

The idea of a God of Love isn't new. Ikhnaton, king of Egypt more than 3,300 years ago, whose spirit is in me, said what I am saying now. So I am not breaking new ground, just reinforcing old truths.

When it comes to the truth of your own journey, I hope your trip is as rewarding as mine has been. I hope you believe as I do that our time in the Book of

Life is the most fascinating chapter. I hope you find that gold white light of God's Love and Truth inside you as I have found it in me. I hope you ascend to a high level of conscious contact with God. And I hope one day to meet you in the place of love God has reserved for us in Heaven.

I have a few closing words for you. I love the self God has created me to be. I love the God of Love who revealed Himself to me. I love the Revelations from God that came through me at Monadnock. And I love you. May God bless you and keep you. May you truly love yourself. May you overflow with love for others. And may you express your love and gratitude to the God of Love.

The end?

Let's think of it as a new beginning.

St. Francis picture & unicorn
Shiva, C.G. Jung, etc.

Horus papyrus & Horus tote bag
from Egypt

About the Author

Tom O'Connell is a health writer, lecturer, and educator. He wrote the *Cape Cod Times* column "On Addiction" (1986-98), and is now a Health/Lifestyle columnist for the on-line *Cape Cod Journal*. He teaches writing at Cape Cod Community College, and is listed in *Who's Who in the East.*

He is a member of the Cape Cod Writers' Center and served as president of the New England Chapter of American Medical Writers Association. For eight years he was national correspondent for *The US Journal of Drug & Alcohol Dependence.*

At Boston's Channel 25, his show "It's Your Life" explored health and spirituality. On Cape Cod's C3TV he produced "Understanding Addiction."

Before becoming an independent health writer he was CEO of Massachusetts Safety Council, and executive director of three other organizations involving long-term health care, public housing, and the auto industry. His work gave him deep insights into the workings of "the world."

Tom O'Connell holds a BA degree *cum laude* in History & Government from Boston College, and an MA in History from The Graduate School at Boston University. He is a Christian and Secular Franciscan.

Enlightening Reading by Tom O'Connell
Health/Spirituality/Personal Growth/Recovery
Published by Sanctuary Unlimited

__The Monadnock Revelations:
   A Spiritual Memoir

An inspirational journal on the author's life before experiencing God in the Monadnock Mountains on September 5, 1985...his hour of channeling the voice of the God of Love...divine revelations...his life since that special hour. ISBN 0-9620318-5-2 $15

__Danny The Prophet: A Fantastic Adventure

An unforgettable novel about a man reluctant to be the last prophet. A trip into another dimension with a politician, a sage, an angel, perilous adventures, and divine revelations. ISBN 0-9620318-4-4 $12

__The Odd Duck:
   A Story for Odd People of All ages

A cheerful, inspiring fable for all "adult children." A lost duck raised in a chicken coop feels odd. After an identity crisis, she begins a quest for self-worth and healthy, lasting love. ISBN 0-9620318-3-6 $7

__Improving Intimacy: 10 Powerful Strategies

A look at spiritually-based intimacy, with strategies for enhancing one's close relationships. Insights on addictive relating, control, listening, communication, conflict...and more. ISBN 0-9620318-2-8 $7

__Addicted? A Guide to Understanding Addiction

Explains addiction's causes, effects, and recovery process. Covers alcohol, other drugs, food, gambling, sex. Gives useful tips. ISBN 0-9620318-0-1 $19

(Visit your local bookseller or use this order form)

Sanctuary Unlimited
PO Box 25
Dennisport, Massachusetts 02639, USA

Please send me the books I am listing below.
I expect delivery in 3-4 weeks.

Name:_____

Phone:_____

Address:_____

City:_____State:_____ZIP:_____

No. of Items	Title	Price
_____		$_____
_____		$_____
_____		$_____
_____		$_____
Total price_____		$_____
Add $2.00 postage/hdlg first item		$_____
and $1.00 each additional item		$_____
Mass. residents: add 5% sales tax		$_____
Enclose check/money order: Total		$_____

(No cash or C.O.D., please)
Prices subject to change without notice.
<5% of $15 = .75 $7 = .35 $19 = .95 $20 = 1.00>

Reader Opinion Survey

Please tear out this page, give us your comments, and forward to...
   Sanctuary Unlimited
   PO Box 25
   Dennisport, MA 02639

Subject: THE MONADNOCK REVELATIONS

Here are my comments on Tom O'Connell's book, *The Monadnock Revelations: (Print or type)*

_____
_____
_____
_____
_____
_____

(Please sign _and_ print your name)
Signed:_____
Address:_____
City:_____State:_____Zip:_____
Occupation:_____

Please check one:
   ___You may quote me for marketing and advertising, and in testimonial pages inserted into future copies of the book.
   ___Please limit use of my comments to anonymous quotes such as "One reader said...."
   Thank you for your cooperation.

Catch and Release

~

Essential Prose Series 198

Canada Council   Conseil des Arts
for the Arts   du Canada

ONTARIO ARTS COUNCIL
CONSEIL DES ARTS DE L'ONTARIO
an Ontario government agency
un organisme du gouvernement de l'Ontario

Canadä

Guernica Editions Inc. acknowledges the support of the Canada Council
for the Arts and the Ontario Arts Council. The Ontario Arts Council
is an agency of the Government of Ontario.

We acknowledge the financial support of the Government of Canada.